Homing in on Houseplants

Also by Daphne Ledward and published by Robson Books

Simply Gardening

The Awkward Spot

The Big Cover-Up

Homing in on Houseplants

Choosing and Caring — the Right Plant for the Right Place

Daphne Ledward

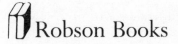

Robson Books

Colour photographs by John Hands
Line drawings by the author

First published in Great Britain in 1989 by Robson Books Ltd,
Bolsover House, 5–6 Clipstone Street, London W1P 7EB

British Library Cataloguing in Publication Data
Ledward, Daphne
    Homing in on Houseplants.
    1. Indoor plants. Cultivation
    I. Title
    635.9'65

ISBN 0 86051 602 4

Photoset by Rowland Phototypesetting Ltd,
Bury St Edmunds, Suffolk.
Printed in Great Britain by St Edmundsbury Press Ltd,
Bury St Edmunds, Suffolk.

Contents

Acknowledgements

The author wishes to thank Reinhard Biehler, Jim Jack and the staff of Baytree Nurseries, Weston, Spalding, Lincs, and Bruce and Aileen Rainsbury, The Nurseries, Cowbit, Spalding, Lincs, for allowing her and John Hands to cause chaos while taking the photographs.

Introduction

This, I hope, is a book about houseplants with a slightly different slant. Any gardening series would be incomplete without something on that branch of horticulture that seems to cause more tears than any other, but there are so many excellent books on the cultivation of these tantalizing and frustrating plants that I doubt if I could add anything new or useful to what there is around at present. I was even tempted to exclude altogether from this series this particular form of cultivation, and yet, as success with houseplants does seem to elude so many people, there must be a need for something which would attempt to shed some light on the situation, so to speak, and that is what I hope this book will do to some extent.

Working on as many gardening programmes and advice columns as I do, three things are clear – there are very few who would not under any circumstances give room to a houseplant of some kind, a large proportion of the population loves them, and yet there seems to be a blind spot in the majority of us which is unable to get the best out of them. It would be a sorry old outdoor landscape where all the plants were in the same state of well-being as what most of us are prepared to tolerate in a position of prominence in our homes! The other surprising fact which emerges as I talk to people about their struggles with houseplants is how many are happy to try, try and try again regardless of the number of times some choice (and often expensive) specimen has 'folded up' on them. I admire their fortitude, as impatience (and impecunity) would curtail my perseverance.

There is no doubt about it, the houseplant industry in the United Kingdom is booming (or is it blooming?), even though we are well behind our mainland European neighbours in the importance that plants play in the overall furnishing of our homes. We are even beginning to develop a thriving demand for home-produced house-plants, in contrast to a few years ago, when the largest part of the stock which eventually ended up in our living rooms was imported from the Continent. This reversal is due in many respects to British growers having studied the propagation techniques of other successful houseplant-producing countries, but another factor is the high degree of science and technology which is playing an increasing part in the mass-production of plants, both for indoor and outdoor cultivation.

For example, take the ever-popular African violet (*Saintpaulia ionantha*). At one time there were only two methods of increasing stock: by seed, which produced variable and unpredictable plants, and by taking leaf cuttings. For true-to-type plants, one had to use the leaf-cutting method, and this is still used widely today. This involves severing a leaf of the right maturity, dipping the attached stem into a rooting compound to speed up the formation of roots, and inserting it into a cutting compost for about half the length of the stem. Eventually new plantlets form around the base of the stem, and when these are large enough to handle they are separated and potted-up individually. Now, although this is a perfectly acceptable method, there are two drawbacks which were insurmountable until the dawn of the era of 'test tube' cultivation: the material for propagation was limited, and saleable plants took time to produce.

In recent years, however, the process generally known as 'tissue culture' has revolutionized the mass propagation of many plants, the African violet being a good example. Small pieces of suitable tissue are removed from the parent plant, which is usually selected for outstanding characteristics, health and vigour, and are grown on in a special nutrient jelly to give a large amount of the same type of tissue. By separating this, and again growing on the small portions, you can see that, in quite a short time, a very great quantity of the same material can be obtained. By then dividing it up yet again, but this time growing the small pieces on in a jelly with different nutrients, the tissue can be encouraged to turn into baby versions of the original parent, which at a certain stage are potted-on to grow up into new plants.

It is clear that, using this method, a great number of new plants can be grown from a very small amount of propagation material, thereby cutting down the number of stock plants required and speeding up the manufacture of saleable stock. Provided good quality plants were used in the first place, the tissue-culture method will ensure that first-rate youngsters are obtained and, in addition, give plants which are more even of form. The technique has been applied to a wide range of species with success commercially, but although do-it-yourself kits have been marketed for amateurs from time to time, there are problems associated with attempting tissue culture in the home, and as yet it is very much a 'high-tech' laboratory process.

Another reason why it has become possible to produce houseplants which are healthy (at the time they leave the nursery, at any rate!) and at a viable price is the way automation has cut down handling and taken the guesswork out of the glasshouse environment. The biggest house-plant producers in Britain have introduced computerized watering and ventilation systems which even enrich the air with carbon dioxide if necessary to improve growth, artificial daylight and darkness to retard or bring forward flowering to give us flowering pot-plants out of season, moving benches to reduce handling, heated beds to speed up rooting, and many other devices for ensuring that their products are in the peak of health for the duration of their stay at the nursery. A visit to a wholesale houseplant nursery is quite an experience – and can be quite unpleasant environmentally, as the air is often more humid than we like. I always extend some sympathy to the people who have to work permanently in such an atmosphere, as it can be extremely tiring. Knowing the fate that most of the happy, flourishing plants there are ultimately destined for, I often feel quite sorry for these, too!

So, if everything in the hot-house garden is lovely at this stage, what goes wrong? Why do so many houseplants end up on the compost heap? I suppose it would be easy to blame the eventual owner, and it is, admittedly, quite often his or her fault, though not necessarily always. It is not always appreciated that, between the propagating nursery and the ultimate purchaser, there can be many middlemen – usually, it has to be said, quite efficient, but somewhere along the line, generally near the end, there can be a weak link in the chain.

Many of the big houseplant-producing nurseries only have respon-sibility for their charges while they are quite small, and at the point when they require their first or second potting-up they are sold to other nurseries who put them into bigger pots and grow them on until they are ready to be resold to a variety of retail outlets. Some firms only deal with one potting-on, others will grow the same specimens for several years until they have become an attractive, tempting, and usually outrageously expensive tub full of weeping fig, palm, yucca, or whatever. When the amount of care, attention and handling that is attached to one of these large specimen houseplants is considered, it is understandable that you are sometimes expected to part with around £100 for the privilege of having one of these to grace your home.

The nurseries which grow houseplants on into saleable specimens are mainly wholesalers themselves, and it is not often that the general public can obtain their plants at this point in the handling chain. It is mostly the garden centre, larger store, supermarket, corner shop or market stallholder who are the customers, and at the risk of offending some sellers of houseplants, it has to be admitted that this is frequently where the problems arise.

Some plant producers will not sell to retail outlets whom they feel are unable to maintain their plants in the same condition as they were when they left the nursery, and some larger chain stores ensure that the members of their staff who have responsibility for houseplants are trained in both their care and basic customer information. Sadly, however, there are many others – including, I notice, some of the best 'High Street' names – who have no idea how to cope with these living charges, and they are frequently displayed in quite unsuitable positions, for example, a dark corner at the back of the shop or a baking, sunny window. I cringe when I see how many of these plants are lovingly bought by the unsuspecting, sickness and disease having already gained a foothold even before they leave the shop. Another failing of the untrained assistant is the inability to water correctly, and if the plant has been drowned or, conversely, has not received a drop since it left the wholesaler, it is unlikely to behave itself when you get it home.

There is, of course, a bright side to every situation, and this kind of treatment has resulted in a new type of indoor gardener appearing – the one who can't resist a challenge, and searches 'bargain displays' and rubbish heaps for the most moribund specimens, carrying them home to the bosom of the family and lavishing loving care on them until a recovery is effected. I must say that, whereas most people would have neither the aptitude nor the patience for this kind of thing, the person who gets pleasure out of saving sick plants usually succeeds in re-vitalizing their charges, and must get much satisfaction out of doing so. I should warn, however, that strictly speaking this is not a particularly good idea, especially if you have a good collection of houseplants, as sometimes you can bring pests and diseases into the house on neglected plants, which can decimate a display very quickly.

For the majority of us who are not lucky enough to have access to a supply of houseplants directly from the nursery, the best place to purchase them from is probably the garden centre with an area specially set aside for this purpose. Even then, though, you have to be careful, because (and this amazes me) some garden centres still do not appreciate that houseplants need careful handling.

The prospective purchaser can do much to ascertain whether the centre is really clued up by looking at the type of position in which the houseplants are kept. Ideally it should be a glasshouse-type structure, with blinds or other shading in summer to protect against scorch and adequate, thermostatically controlled heating when necessary. Ventilation is usually not a problem, as the garden centre proprietor is likely to pay attention to this for the comfort of the customers! The houseplants should be stood on damp capillary matting or other moisture-retaining material unless they are very large and are in very big containers. Plants in flower and those with variegated leaves should, if possible, be given a brighter situation than all-green foliage subjects. The most efficient centres will have a thermometer in an obvious position, to indicate to them, as much as to you, if everything is well as far as temperature is concerned.

Anybody buying a houseplant, wherever they are purchasing it from, should check it carefully for any obvious signs of stress. I would be very dubious of any retailer displaying a large number of plants with brown or shrivelled patches on the leaves, yellowing, over- or underwatering, or those in urgent need of repotting – this can be spotted by turning the pot over and examining the base; a few white roots beginning to appear are not a bad sign, but a tangled mat of dried-up, brown ones are a clear indication that the plant should have received attention some time ago, and could be difficult to grow on once it was home. However, even the best centres can have an odd one which is not quite up to standard, so it is advisable to be just as careful if the whole house looks flourishing.

The place to give a miss as far as the purchase of houseplants is concerned is the cold corner shop or greengrocer's, where plants with their origins in the tropics are left outside in all weathers, and this applies even more to the outdoor market stall. Summer is not so bad – in fact some plants will even appreciate the fresh air – but in winter the temperature is far too cold for most of them to be given the outdoor treatment, particularly as they will possibly be put back into a warmer position at night. The widely fluctuating temperatures can be as lethal as over-low ones alone.

It would appear from what I have just said then that, provided you pick a houseplant with healthy leaves, which is correctly potted in what appears to be good compost, from an outlet where it received impeccable attention and where its neighbours were bursting with good health, you can't go wrong. Unfortunately, this is by no means the case. Because I began by describing the things that can cause a houseplant to fail which are no fault of the ultimate owner, it can give the impression that it is unusual for the owner to be the culprit. The majority of deaths are, in fact, caused by the plant owner who does not understand the plant sufficiently to give it what it needs.

The attitude of the home-owner towards the plants in the house is frequently quite different from his or her attitude towards the plants in the garden. The garden, it is felt, is a place for plants. If you want an 'ornament', then you add a statue, bird table or stone urn. A house – and into that category come, of course, bungalows, flats, bed-sitters, even caravans or barges, if you like – is looked on as a place for people, aided in their activities and creature comforts by furniture of one sort and another. In this case, if an ornament is required, what is so often decided upon is the poor old houseplant. As this is to complement the furnishings, style or function of the particular room for which it is destined, the personal requirements of the plant take a back seat. More important is the shape, colour or form, the position it is required for, and even, in these days of relative affluence, the size of the specimen. I am constantly amazed at the cost of some of the casualties I am consulted about, which were bought for totally unsuitable places. I suppose some of the trouble is that houseplants, by the time they arrive in our homes, are so far removed from their natural origins that it is difficult to feel that they simply are just living things, which evolved in a particular place and because of their evolution have specific requirements to enable them to flourish in that specific location. To thrive anywhere else, those conditions have to be reproduced as nearly as possible.

This acclimatization is also the reason why it is often possible for a younger plant, providing it is well enough established to cope with some alteration in its environment, to re-establish itself better in the home than a very large one, which has been given nearly ideal conditions for a much longer time. The younger plant, after perhaps some initial shock, will (if it does not die, of course!) re-adjust to the new environment, its own system adapting slightly to its surroundings.

Home design has become so important of late that you tend to find an increasing number of articles in popular magazines, and even sections of the houseplant area of garden centres, devoted to suggestions for certain rooms of the house. Plants for the hall, the bathroom, the kitchen, the living room, the dining room and even the bedroom are suggested, and while most ideas are fairly sound, for the inexperienced houseplant owner to stick rigidly to them can be misleading, as the plan usually assumes that *all* bathrooms are warm and steamy, *all* kitchens are bright and warm, *all* living rooms are centrally heated, *all* dining rooms only have reasonable warmth when there is a dinner party, *all* halls are cold and dark, *all* bedrooms are of even temperature, or whatever conception of home life it is that the person compiling the collection has. And yet each home is so different from the next that these are unwise assumptions to make. I know many living rooms where only a coal fire is used and where plants thrive because the air is less dry than if central heating were installed, bathrooms where it is barely comfortable to clean the teeth, kitchens which are large, dark and only warm up once a week when the Sunday roast is cooked, bright, snug halls, and so on, where ideas for the average home would be quite unsuitable.

To be a successful houseplant owner, the first point to remember is that it is the plant which is important, not the piece of furniture which could be improved by standing something on it, nor the dull corner which is just crying out for improvement. Undeniably, well-placed plants can improve the decor of a room phenomenally, but it is a sad waste of a plant, and foolish extravagance, to put plants in situations where they just will not grow, merely because something would look nice there – unless, of course, you subscribe to the increasingly popular theory that most houseplants are expendable, more like a longer lasting bunch of flowers than a permanent feature, and can be replaced once they start to look unhappy. If you have a greenhouse or other light spot which you know plants thrive in, you can remove them from the unsuitable area for a period of recuperation if you feel you must have a particular plant in a particular place regardless of preferences, but it really is better in the first place to get your plant and your room living happily together.

I am going to make a suggestion here which will make many readers throw up their hands in horror, and that is, not to condemn out-of-hand the use of artificial houseplants. These have come a very long way from the crude plastic imitations of a few years ago, and the best imitations are extremely difficult to distinguish from the real thing. I even have to feel the leaves myself sometimes to tell the difference, especially with some of the more exotic species. I am not an advocate of the single silk croton stuck on top of the television, but I have seen groups of artificial houseplants used effectively in certain situations, and even a mixture of dark-leaved real houseplants, like the weeping fig (*Ficus benjamina*), Swiss cheese plant (*Monstera deliciosa*) or castor oil plant (*Fatsia japonica*), and variegated silk ones where the light level would have been too low to support the real versions of the latter successfully.

There are two ways in which houseplants co-exist in the modern household. By far the most likely spot to find them, even in these 'stylish' days when it is frowned upon by exponents of perfect decor, is adorning the windowsills. From the houseplants' point of view, this is probably the best place for them, as light levels drop off dramatically the further away from the window you go, and with luck you can pick the sill to suit the plants – north-facing for those which scorch in sun, east-facing for those requiring some bright light but not during the hottest parts of the day, and south- and west-facing for certain plants which really revel in hot, bright sunshine. You may find you need to swap windowsills at certain times of the year – those plants which will not tolerate sun in summer may like lighter conditions in winter, for example. Windowsills are not the problem in winter that they used to be, now we are more conscious of draught and heat-loss. Most houseplants object to draughts, which are far more harmful to them than consistently low temperatures, and in very cold spells the area against a single-glazed window may be too chilly for many plants, but it should be remembered that *all* window areas become very cold when the curtains are drawn at night, and so even if the panes are double-glazed it is advisable to move plants on windowsills into the body of the room on a winter's evening.

The more fashionable indoor gardener, as I have already mentioned, uses houseplants as room features in the same way as you would use a piece of furniture or pottery that is more ornamental than useful. For the right effect, the plant or plants have to be large enough and bold enough to be noticed, but not so overpowering as to make everyday living in the room fraught with difficulty. A well-shaped, well-grown specimen plant can be just the thing for a bare surface, but often the best way of introducing plants is to group them together, contrasting different habits, forms, leaf colours and textures just as you would when planning a shrubbery. Not only can this produce some dramatic effects if done properly, but it is much easier to keep the plants in good heart as, massed together, the moisture from the leaves (transpiration) raises the humidity in the vicinity of the plants, creating a beneficial microclimate of moister air, a particularly desirable feature in a centrally heated room with a dry atmosphere.

Plants can be grouped together in their individual pots, but it is really better to group them in an outer container filled with moist peat, perlite, 'Hortag' (a volcanic gravel-like substance which is very absorbent) or similar, which will also help to keep the surrounding air moist. Several plants can be put directly into a large container of compost if you intend the display to be more or less permanent; some of these containers have quite ingenious self-watering devices which help to prevent over- or underwatering.

When choosing plants for permanent groupings, it is essential to combine together those which require the same conditions. It is not a good idea to incorporate variegated forms in a dull corner, as they will lose their colour, although it is effective to combine green leaves and variegated ones where the light is good enough. When plants are growing in one large container, if there is good natural daylight, gaps can be left where temporary flowering subjects can be added and removed, complete with pot, to introduce some different effects. Many flowering houseplants last longest where the temperature is not too high, so for the greatest benefit this should also be borne in mind. It is advisable to check on the temperature requirements of all houseplants before grouping them together, in case you are trying to mix those with extremes of preferences, although massing them together will help certain plants to tolerate a wider range, especially if the watering is watched carefully.

In some 'activity' rooms – for example, the kitchen, utility room, bathroom or workroom – having a lot of plants taking up valuable work surface area, floor space or light may be undesirable, and in cases such as these it may be better to abandon the idea of groups or free-standing specimens in favour of a trailing or semi-weeping plant in a hanging basket or pot. This type of plant will also need good light, so should be sited quite near the window. If you intend to drive a hook into the ceiling – and there are several attractive ornamental ones available at garden centres these days – you must make absolutely sure that you are fixing it to the floor joist or ceiling joist and not the plasterboard, or it may not be just the plant that falls down!

Another point to remember is that hot air rises, and so if the room in which you intend to suspend plants is very warm, you should steer away from subjects like ivies and many ferns which will turn brown under such conditions, choosing those which will tolerate a fair amount of warmth. In the following chapters I will be recommending some trailing plants for different temperature levels and various degrees of light.

The greatest revolution in indoor gardening in recent years is the increasing popularity of the modern conservatory. This began to make its appearance in the Sixties with the garden room, often prefabricated, which was essentially an extension of the rather cramped living area found in many homes built after the Second World War. It was more often used as another room, with any plants growing therein being incidental, but a decade later the sun or garden room had evolved into a glazed structure with a sloping, transparent roof resembling more a lean-to greenhouse than a conventional room. This seemed to begin a trend where the structure's primary function was to grow plants, recreation and entertaining being more of a secondary consideration. The lean-to greenhouse has now developed into full-blown Victorian-style conservatories, much more elaborate, usually many-sided, affairs, which seem to be springing up everywhere. They can be used to such good effect on traditional and older buildings, but look somewhat incongruous added onto – as is so often the case – the somewhat austere lines of the modern, functional style of home!

The main advantage of this type of plant house is, however, the increased height at the apex, enabling much larger and more interesting plants to be grown in addition to those normally associated with the 'sun-lounge'. It is also usually easier to grow plants happily as the light is better and humidity can be increased if necessary by 'damping down', if suitable furniture is used. Because there are so many of these extensions about nowadays, I have included two chapters at the end of the book on this subject, one for the warmer conservatory, and one for that which is unheated or just heated enough to keep the frost out; these chapters are intended to provide suggestions to supplement the usual plants grown under glass.

For those not lucky enough to own a conservatory, and those who have not yet been tempted by the idea and yet have difficulty in growing any houseplant well, I have also included a chapter on bottle gardens and the like, as, if you think about it, these are really only greenhouses in miniature, and there are undeniably some homes which are so dry and hot that this is probably the best solution. My sitting room is a typical example of this kind of situation: it is low and not large, and the multi-fuel stove which provides the central heating resides there, so from October to May the room is unsuitably warm. The windows face north and south, but are very small, so light levels are poor except in the immediate vicinity of the glass. However, the sills are wide, and a bottle garden – placed on the north-facing sill in summer and on the south one in winter – simply romps away. Although it is warm, the air is humid, and the extra glass prevents chilling in cold weather.

This book, then, is not intended as a cultural reference book for every type of plant you are likely to grow in the home. It is my recognition of the fact that houseplants *are* part of the home, and therefore deserve to receive as much attention, and should look as good, as all the other features which go to make up the total effect. In the same way as when I consider a garden, then, I have taken different kinds of conditions where plants may be required as part of the 'furnishings' and made suggestions for successful subjects. The number of species is, naturally, limited, because if I have any doubt as to whether or not a particular thing would thrive, I have purposely excluded it. You can be reasonably sure, therefore, that providing you stick to the situation a plant prefers, it should behave itself reasonably well. It is not necessarily the most obscure subject which will give you the best effect, and listing species which are only obtainable from a limited number of nurseries could cause frustration, so all my recommendations should be obtained without difficulty from reliable sources.

A word about containers

There is an enormous range of pots, troughs, tubs, stands and other containers around, and it is tempting to spend a great deal of money without thinking the subject through properly, so maybe, if you have no fixed ideas, a word of advice could be useful.

At one time all pot plants were grown in clay pots, using a compost containing a large amount of loam (good soil). Loam-based compost needs a different watering technique – generally not as often as the faster-drying peat-based ones – and the clay pot, which absorbs moisture, is helpful in maintaining the correct amount of water in the growing medium, as excess tends to evaporate through the sides. When plastic pots gradually began to supersede the clay sorts, many gardeners who were used to the latter experienced difficulty in getting the watering right and waterlogging problems were likely to occur. However, since the advent of some excellent peat-based composts, including ones specially formulated for use with houseplants, these troubles have largely disappeared, particularly as far as a new generation of gardeners is concerned which has experienced nothing else except plastic pots and peat-based composts.

The reason for my giving you a 'potted' history of pots is to help point out that possibly the ideal container for houseplants is the plastic plant pot itself, especially where smaller plants are involved. It is designed to have optimum proportions which have been proved to do best for most species. It is also of an unobtrusive black or brown colour – after all, it is the plants which are the stars of the show, not the containers, and elaborate plant-pot holders seldom contribute anything extra, particularly when many plants are grouped together.

Using an outer container can have the advantage that it can be filled with moisture-absorbing material as previously described, which will help to keep the air around the plant humid, but as many decorative pots do not have drainage holes, it is all too easy to overwater the compost and drown the roots because the excess water cannot drain away or be seen to be standing in the outer pot, thus preventing the compost from drying out gradually. If a pot with drainage holes stands in a saucer, it can be spotted immediately if excess water is standing around the base, and it can be poured away before it does damage. I strongly recommend that where a group of plants is planted in a large container, adequate visible drainage is provided, as it is extremely difficult to know whether you have got the watering right otherwise, and the bottom half of the compost can be permanently bone-dry or saturated without your knowing it. Moisture meters are available, but often do not have a long enough probe to reach the base of a deep container. Having an outer holder can be beneficial, though, in sunny positions as it gives extra protection from heat at the roots.

Ideally, a container should be of an unobtrusive pattern and design. Ceramic, brass, copper, cane, wicker, wrought iron and good quality plastic are all acceptable – a well thought-out arrangement will, in time, conceal much of the holder anyway. Pot and other container sizes are quite important – they should not be too small or the plant will be top-heavy and need constant watering and repotting, but, as well as looking out-of-proportion, plants seldom do well in containers that are too large for them (that is, more than one or two sizes larger than the one they were in previously).

The art of correct potting will be looked at in more detail in the following chapter.

Keeping houseplants happy

Caring for a houseplant begins the very moment you acquire it. Unless you receive it as a gift, this usually means when you have checked it for health and carried it carefully to the till. Most nurseries will wrap it for you with a special cellophane wrapping or place it in a paper sleeve – not only does this protect the plant from damage, it also helps to keep the temperature even around it until you get it home. You should try to ensure that from the minute the plant leaves the shop it does not suffer any sudden extremes of temperature – very cold in winter or very hot in summer – so this could mean leaving your plant purchases till last if you are on a shopping expedition. If you feel you must buy from a store which does not offer a wrapping facility, you ought to provide one for yourself – a polythene carrier bag is better than nothing.

The plant should be kept upright during the journey home. Most well-grown specimens have sufficient root systems to bind the compost, but some younger ones may have loose material in the pot, and the whole affair could drop to bits if the plant falls over. Root disturbance at this stage is just what the poor thing does not need – it will have enough stress in the weeks that follow without another unnecessary one.

It pays to have done your homework in advance, finding out the conditions a particular species likes before you buy it, but I suppose nearly all of us are tempted to buy houseplants on impulse, so this is where a little information is helpful immediately the plant arrives in your home. In my suggestions for particular places (see pages 41–83) I have given brief cultural details, but if you want more information, it is wise to invest in one of my recommendations for further reading on page 128.

The great urge now is to site the plant in its permanent location, but if you are not able to reproduce exactly the conditions it likes in that spot, you really ought to find somewhere in the house which is as near as possible to these preferences until it has got over the trauma of moving. Unless something has gone drastically wrong before you bought it, or while you were transporting it home, you will not know for some time whether it has settled in with you. If, after several weeks, it does not appear to have problems, you could then try it in its permanent place. It should readapt without trouble, unless you are attempting too extreme a change, in which case you have got the wrong plant for the chosen spot anyway.

Unless you have obtained something which is crying out for re-potting, which you really ought to have thought twice about buying anyway, as this is one indication that it was not receiving as much care as it ought to have had, do try to resist the temptation to repot it immediately. This advice also applies if you are making a permanent arrangement in a large tub – pop the plants into their positions in it temporarily without removing the pot, until they are settled.

The aspects of regular houseplant care which seem to cause the most worry are watering, feeding and repotting, so I shall now deal with these techniques in some detail.

Watering

Most people tend to kill their houseplants with kindness, and watering too much is one of the commonest causes of failure. It is difficult to generalize about water requirement, because all houseplants are living things with their own characteristics, but it is reasonably safe to say that, with a few exceptions (which I have listed in a section for people who just can't stop overwatering their houseplants), it is better to underwater slightly than to overwater habitually.

The reason why plants, unless they are specially adapted for semi-aquatic conditions, will eventually die if the compost is too wet is root failure. Most plants need air around the roots to function correctly; where the compost is sodden there is little air and the roots are unable to perform their task of taking up plant foods in solution properly. The compost becomes sour, the roots start to die from their delicate ends, and soon the visible parts of the plant begin to show signs that they are not getting what they should be receiving from below. It is possible to save a plant which has been overwatered for a short time, but a regularly drowned one will almost certainly die.

Signs of overwatering are poor growth, leaves turning yellow with brown tips and soft, rotten patches, young and old leaves dropping off and, where appropriate, mouldy flowers. If you turn the plant out of its pot, the compost will be wet, the roots soggy and disintegrating and, in very bad cases, there is a disgusting smell.

21

If the plant is a mature one, it is sometimes possible to rescue it if the roots are cut back to any which are firm, with white centres, and then it should be repotted in a good houseplant compost which is just damp. It may be necessary to use a pot which is several sizes smaller after this treatment – on no account should it be replanted in too much compost or this is likely to turn sour before the roots have recovered and grown into it fully.

Underwatering is usually indicated by wilting leaves and stems, brown edges to the leaves, yellowing and falling older leaves, and flowers (if any) which mature and fade quickly. The remedy is, of course, to increase the amount of water given, but as you can see from my description, it isn't quite as simple as that, as certain symptoms are common to both conditions – wilting, yellowing and browning, for example. This is where, if you are not experienced with houseplants, a root examination is vital, when it is obvious that a dry, dusty rootball indicates underwatering, and a soggy, stinking mess indicates too much.

Watering is definitely an art, acquired over many years of owning and observing houseplants. As I mentioned earlier, there are devices which can help you to assess whether you need to water or not. One is the battery-operated electronic water meter, which has a probe that is pushed into the soil; a dial indicates whether watering is needed or not. This is fine for all plants which have normal requirements, but you have to use some common sense with those which should be kept very dry or very wet. Phostrogen produce a handy and inexpensive cardboard indicator, which is inserted into the compost; it turns from yellow to green when the plant is damp enough, and back to yellow again when it needs watering again. This, I find, does tend to get less accurate after a while, and should be replaced regularly.

The frequency with which you water depends on many factors. Plants in a warm room will need watering more often than plants in a cool one; those in a sunny position will require more water than those in shade. In summer you may need to water several times a week; in winter in a cool position plants may only need water once a month – or even less for certain species. The golden rule is to check before you water, then apply a good amount. A daily dribble is highly undesirable.

People who have cultivated houseplants for a number of years develop an instinct about watering. When clay pots were widely used, the grower could tell from tapping the side whether they needed watering or not – a dull sound indicated that the compost was still damp, a ringing one meant that it was dry enough to need watering again. Of course, you cannot do that with plastic pots, but after a while you get to know from the weight of them whether they are wet or dry – a heavy pot means the compost has plenty of water in it, a light one says to you that it has dried out, and a very light one tells you it is high time you got the watering can out!

Most houseplants need watering when the compost at the top has started to dry out, but not for so long that the whole rootball has become dehydrated. With a few exceptions, if the compost is damp on the surface, it will not need watering as it will be quite damp enough underneath. At the stage when the top is just dry, I find the best way to water is with a small watering can which is specially designed for use with houseplants, giving enough for the surplus to run through the bottom. This is allowed to drain for an hour or so, and then poured away to prevent waterlogging.

When a plant is getting to the stage of being repotted, however, water can often run straight out without wetting the roots and what is left of the compost. In this case, if repotting is not possible for some reason, I find the answer is to leave the plant soaking up to the pot rim in a bowl of tepid water for about an hour before removing it and letting it drain thoroughly – it should not be put back in its outer container before the excess water has run off.

You will often hear the advice that some houseplants need watering from the base – which generally means pouring water into the saucer until it has been absorbed. This method is usually recommended for plants with fleshy crowns, corms which can collect water in the top, and those species with furry leaves. The reason why it is considered wiser to water from the bottom is that if water falls on the crown or leaves, or lodges in the corm, rotting can occur. If top watering worries you, then watering from the base is the answer, but it is better to submerge the pot as I have already described, rather than trickle water into the saucer; this latter method makes it almost impossible to tell whether water has soaked far enough up and into the rootball, and underwatering can occur. Furthermore, it is tempting to leave the plants standing in water longer than necessary if water is poured into the saucer in situ, which is most certainly not a good idea!

If you really feel that you cannot cope accurately with watering, then maybe self-watering pots are the answer, but the drawback with these is that they tend to keep the compost damp all the time, and a lot of houseplants prefer the compost to dry out somewhat between watering. The same applies to self-watering devices and capillary matting, which are often used in a greenhouse or conservatory environment, though these can be a blessing when you go away for more than a week or so, especially in summer. There is a big drawback in respect of self-watering pots in that they cannot distinguish between winter and summer. Plants need a resting period in the darker months of the year, and to help them to do this they should be kept much drier as they are not in active growth, even if the room temperature is high. There are far more plant fatalities in winter than in summer, nearly always connected with overwatering.

One point that is seldom appreciated is that it is not always beneficial to use water straight from the tap. In certain areas, additives such as chlorine can have a moderately detrimental effect on house-plants, and many are not keen on the highly alkaline drinking water found in a lot of places. Lime in the water can build up in the compost to affect not only lime-haters like azaleas but quite a wide range of subjects. However, soft water can also be a problem. Collecting rainwater in a butt is fine for use on larger specimens and outdoor plants, but does itself contain impurities, either from the atmosphere or from the material of which the roof is constructed. Water butts can also introduce diseases, especially if they are not cleaned out and disinfected regularly. If you have a refrigerator which produces 'distilled' water when defrosted, this can be collected and used on houseplants as it is quite neutral and contains no impurities at all, but there is seldom enough of this, especially if you are a houseplant fanatic.

My advice to most people is to continue to use water out of the tap unless you see positive signs of deterioration – this usually manifests itself as yellowing and general discoloration of the leaves. Many modern houseplant feeds now contain the trace elements which are 'locked up' in the compost and therefore denied to the plants, by the excess lime in the soil. These trace elements, such as iron, magnesium, manganese, copper, zinc, boron and molybdenum are added to the fertilizer in a 'chelated' form in which they are still available to the plants, but which prevents them being 'locked up' through the action of the lime. Alternatively, if you are really worried about using tap water, you can collect rain water in a bucket, store it in a clean, dry container, and use it almost immediately. In certain areas, where acid rain is thought to be a problem, it is a good idea to check the pH (acidity/alkalinity) of a sample before using it. You can do this with a simple soil-testing kit.

It is better to take the chill off the water before using it on houseplants. This can be done easiest by leaving a canful indoors, where it will slowly warm to room temperature. If possible, the can should be stood in the same room as the plants for which it is intended, though I realize this is not always practicable. Watering water can also be warmed slightly by adding a little hot to it, but I must stress that it should not itself be hot, or even noticeably warm, just not stone-cold, as the use of very cold water can cause the root growth of many houseplants to suffer a check.

Feeding

All plants, whether they are grown inside the house or in the garden, need certain basic elements in order to survive. The major elements are nitrogen, which promotes healthy top growth, phosphorus, which stimulates strong root growth, and potassium, which 'toughens-up' tissue and encourages flowering. These elements are absorbed by the root hairs of the plant and are generally available in the soil or compost in the form of soluble compounds – nitrates, phosphates and potash. In addition, as mentioned above, plants need very small amounts of certain other elements in order to remain healthy.

An outdoor plant finds much of what it needs in the soil itself, especially if it contains a lot of rotted organic matter. Additional amounts can be supplied when necessary by fertilizers. A houseplant potted in a peat-based compost will find little to nourish it in this medium. Fresh compost has had a fertilizer added to it, but this is in a fairly small amount as overdosing would be toxic, and is generally used up during the first weeks after potting – what is not used up is washed out when watering. After this period, therefore, it becomes necessary during the growing season to supply the required feed in regular amounts.

Under normal circumstances, houseplants are in active growth from the beginning of April to the end of September, during the months of the year with the longest daylength. During this time they will need food to produce strong, disease-resistant growth. During the other

25

months growth slows down to a minimum, and the plant enters into a resting period, which should not be unbalanced by giving fertilizer when it is not required. However, because most places where house-plants reside are as warm in winter, or warmer, than they are in summer, some growth still occurs, even though the days are short. It is a good thing, therefore, to give a very occasional feed to plants so affected throughout the winter, but not so often as to force them into unnecessary growth.

The commonest failing made by most inexperienced houseplant owners when faced with an ailing plant is to give it what it would require if it were bursting with good health. So often I am asked why such and such a plant, showing signs of sickness, failed to improve when given more water, more food and a repotting. Now, I ask you, if you were ill, would you want to be taken out of your familiar bed, stuffed with food, and half-drowned? Extra fertilizer, repotting and, in the vast majority of cases, extra water is the last thing that is wanted. Feeding is necessary to help the plant to grow, and only when it is showing signs of a deficiency disorder, which is uncommon, will a sick plant improve through feeding.

There are a bewildering number of houseplant feeds on the market at present. The ones which have been around the longest are the most basic, and contain the major elements – nitrogen, phosphates and potash, usually in equal amounts. This is fine for the majority of plants, but does not take into account the special requirements certain categories may have. For example, a plant depending for its effect on a strong growth of healthy green leaves needs nitrogen to help it, and a flowering plant will produce more and better blooms if it receives more potash. All fertilizers give the proportions of major and trace elements contained in them on the label – if you think your flowering pot plant could do better with a little more potash, opt for a feed which contains a higher proportion of this.

Providing your plant is getting fed regularly when necessary, it does not pay to be too neurotic, however. All feeds on the shelves of the garden centre come from the major horticultural chemical manufac-turers and have been formulated to be of benefit to a wide range of houseplants. When in doubt choose any one of these; it will last you a long time as only a little is required. One company, Chempak, has produced a different feed for each type of plant – flowering, green leaved, variegated, cacti and orchids – if you have a large number of each sort specialized feeds are worth considering, but if you only have a few general plants you can safely stick to an 'all-rounder'. Houseplant fertilizers with trace elements are a good idea, and those where they have been 'chelated' should be chosen if you water regularly with very hard tap water.

Not only do you find houseplant fertilizers with differing amounts of elements, they also come in different forms to add to the confusion. By far the most common are the liquids, which are added to the water when watering the plant. These are perhaps the easiest to apply, though, because you need very small amounts, the temptation is to overfeed. Remember, *always* read the label; if it says three drops once a week in summer and once a month in winter it means just that, and no more.

Similar to the liquid fertilizer is the soluble one, which comes in powder or crystal form. Again a small amount is added to the watering water, and it dissolves rapidly to make a dilute solution of liquid feed. The water may need to be stirred to make sure it has all dissolved. Like the liquid feed, the tendency is to add a bit more 'for luck'; this should be avoided. It is of more benefit to the plant to feed oftener with a half- or quarter-strength solution than to give a massive dose with a long period in between, but the manufacturer does know his product best, so his recommended dilution rates should be adhered to.

There are a small number of insoluble powder and granular feeds available, though these are less popular. I find they sometimes do not give quite such satisfactory results as they are dependent on watering to get the feed to the roots, and the application of fertilizer can sometimes be uneven, with more at the top where the granules are than at the base of the pot where the roots will absorb them. Also, timing is critical: most of these are designed to release foods over a long period, and so should not be applied too near the time when the plant is starting its annual rest.

Some houseplant foods come in stick or pill form. These are easy to apply (unless the plant needs repotting, when it is almost impossible to push them in, and so is an indication you should be doing something about it) but again tend to give uneven doses of food. The comment about the resting period applies here, too.

In the last few years a whole lot of novel ideas have been developed to make feeding 'easier'. (There is nothing to my mind particularly difficult about adding a few drops of concentrate to a small can of water anyway!) These include leaf-shine wipes impregnated with fertilizer designed to foliar feed as you clean the leaves (quite a good idea, but you cannot feed plants with soft or woolly leaves this way), fertilizer-impregnated mats (I worry slightly about these as I think it could encourage people to leave their plants standing in water far longer than is good for them), and – the latest in the line of easy-feeds – a foliar feed from Vesutor ready-mixed in a hand-operated spray (not an aerosol). This, I think, is the best of the novelties. The food is easy to apply and it does get one into the habit of misting, but you have to be careful where you do it, as you can spoil a table-top with the moisture, so often you need to remove your plants to somewhere more suitable for misting, which can be a bother.

Repotting

To someone without much experience of houseplants, repotting is a mysterious something which has to be done regularly without fail. In fact, putting a houseplant into a larger container is by no means a regular job. In a nutshell, a plant needs repotting when it has outgrown the pot it is in and when it is beginning to show signs of stress. There are many plants, especially flowering ones with bulbous roots, which only need repotting when the roots are splitting the pot, and many other flowering types will produce a profusion of leaves rather than the blooms that are required if repotted too frequently. A plant can be encouraged to flower when it is put under stress – it develops the urge to reproduce itself before it is too late. A pot-bound plant is more under stress than one which is romping away happily in a pot full of well-fertilized compost, and so will produce flowers rather than growth. Certain other plants, among them bromeliads, aspidistra, cacti and succulents, orchids and mother-in-law's tongue (sansevieria) require quite long intervals between repotting.

Signs that a plant needs repotting are a pot packed tightly with roots which have ceased to produce young white growths at their tips, lack of new growth, falling leaves (sometimes, though not always, and as we have seen, this can also be an indication of other cultural disorders), many matted roots coming through the base, and, as mentioned before, a hard compost/root ball which it is impossible to penetrate.

I have already explained that it is bad practice to repot into too large a container as there may be too much compost and added fertilizer for the roots to cope with and dying back of these can occur. As a rule of thumb, very small plants should be potted on into ones which are half a size larger, medium-sized ones into pots a whole size bigger, and very large ones into containers two, or at the most three, sizes bigger. Extremely big specimens are best not disturbed at all; instead the top few inches of compost should be removed annually and replaced with fresh.

Choice of compost can also be confusing. Most houseplants when they leave the nursery, unless they are very large, are potted in a peat-based compost, and this is quite adequate for most houseplants growing in pots up to 10 inches (25 cm) in diameter. However, with mature specimens, especially very tall ones like palms and well-grown yuccas, it is better to use a soil-based compost. There are two reasons for this. One is that a soil-based compost will last much longer before becoming 'played-out', and so the plants can remain in the same medium for several years. The other is that soil is much heavier than peat, which helps to prevent the plant being knocked over inadvertently. The problem is, a plant grown in peat-based compost does not readily re-establish itself into a soil-based one, and vice versa, so it can be a little tricky getting some subjects to make the change. I find that one method which usually works is to mix some peat with the soil-based compost for the first potting into the latter – but this is the *only* time when I would recommend tampering with the formula of composts. Do not use peat-based compost as an additive as you could get the fertilizer balance wrong. John Innes No. 1 is the most suitable compost for smaller plants when you are wanting to transfer them to a soil-based medium; larger ones require John Innes No. 2 and very big ones John Innes No. 3.

Never be tempted to use soil out of the garden for potting up houseplants, however good the quality. It is likely to contain organisms which, although harmless when given free range on a large scale, can be seriously detrimental to houseplants, which are choosy about conditions anyway, when in the close confines of a plant pot.

Three groups of plants will require special composts: cacti, orchids and calcifuges (those which cannot tolerate lime). Cacti need a soil-based compost with plenty of grit and even a few very small stones to aid drainage, or they have a tendency to rot at the base. Orchids require a special orchid compost which used to comprise mainly osmunda fibre but this has been replaced by shredded and chipped bark and sphagnum moss peat, or even rockwool, which is effective, but does not look very nice. Lime-haters like azaleas need an ericaceous medium with no added lime.

Repotting should only take place when the plant is in active growth, that is, during spring and summer – and not too late in the season, or the roots will not have had time to get re-established into the new compost before the resting period, and rotting can occur as a result. If the roots are very congested, it helps to tease them out a little before putting the plant into its new container. The new compost should be firmed lightly but *never* packed solid, or the roots just cannot get into it. A thorough watering is usually enough to finish the job after gently firming with the fingertips. For plants which normally live in quite sunny positions, it pays to let them settle down for a day or two in the shade before returning them to their permanent spots. Once again, never repot a sick plant unless it has been overwatered and the compost is sour, or underwatered through being pot-bound, when it will have a 'washed out' look about it.

There are other important factors which affect the well-being of a houseplant.

Light

Insufficient light is the most frequent cause of a houseplant not looking at its best. All green plants (and that includes variegated ones as well, as they have some green in them) require light such as that from the sun, or a good imitation of it, in order to produce energy to grow. Where light levels are poor, the plant will gradually become weaker, and eventually, if its functions are affected severely enough through lack of light, it will die.

Different plants require different light levels depending on their origins. Those whose ancestors thrived in low light areas, such as those found in tropical and sub-tropical forest situations, will naturally need more shade than those originating in sunny localities, and therefore too much sun would be harmful to tissue unequipped to cope with it. Most flowering houseplants are happiest in good light, where the flower colour and form can develop fully (in the wild they would most likely be relying on their attraction, either visual or through their scent, to birds or insects who would help to pollinate them). Variegated plants tend to lose their variegation in poor light.

Houseplants must, in addition to receiving the right light intensity for their species, also have the correct duration of natural light or bright artificial light containing the correct colours of the spectrum. This should be from 12–16 hours each day; less than this causes a slowing down of food production, which is why plants do not grow very much in winter, even though they may be as warm as in summer. A room with poor natural daylight can be brightened by painting the walls white, as light colours tend to reflect the light.

All plants bend towards the light, though this occurs less if the room walls are painted in a light colour. To prevent the plant becoming misshapen, it should be moved round periodically so the same part of it is not always presented to the light source. This can cause the flower buds of some flowering species to drop, however.

Many flowering plants depend upon day length for their flowering period. For example, African violets need a reasonably long period of daylight, whereas the pot chrysanthemums you can buy in flower at almost any time of the year rely on a short day length – during summer the flower buds are induced artificially by subjecting the plant to an artificially long night. The red 'flowers' of the poinsettia (which are really coloured leaves known as 'bracts') depend on the plant receiving 14 hours of total darkness during the day for 8 weeks. To produce coloured bracts for Christmas, light has to be excluded from the plant in this way for two months from the beginning of September. Even low-level artificial light can have some effect on plants, and in the case of the poinsettia it will prevent the bracts from colouring if the plant is not isolated totally from the light source for its requisite 14 hours each day.

The classic symptoms of a plant receiving too little light are poor, spindly growth, long gaps between leaf joints, small new leaves and pale older ones which fall prematurely. Too much light causes brown, strawy scorch marks, green leaves with a washed-out appearance, shrivelling of the leaves most exposed to the sun, wilting when the sun is at its hottest and damage to the tender new shoots. It is possible to supplement natural daylight with artificial lighting if you must grow plants in places which are too dark to support healthy growth. Special 'Gro-Lux' tubes are available from garden centres stocking greenhouse accessories, or you can use two 40-watt fluorescent tubes – preferably one 'daylight' and one 'warm white'. These are positioned 6–12 inches (15–30 cm) above the plants for flowering houseplants, and 12–24 inches (30–60 cm) above those grown for their foliage.

Plants growing in shaded spots in summer may need more light in winter, when natural light levels fall dramatically. If a plant should start showing signs of receiving too little light, it should be moved nearer a window for the shortest months of the year. Some direct sunlight is unlikely to do any harm, as the sun's rays are too weak to scorch.

Warmth, humidity and ventilation

Plants vary considerably as to their temperature requirements, but the majority of those commonly found in our homes will tolerate a range of from 60–80°F (15–27°C) in summer and 45–65°F (4–18°C) in winter, although they are frequently expected to survive temperatures outside these ranges. It is usual for houseplants to look happiest at lower temperatures, especially if there is adequate light and watering is watched carefully. The reason why many start to show signs of distress in warmer rooms is that the humidity is generally less. Cold air becomes saturated with moisture much more readily than warm air – plants need moisture in the air as well as at the roots to keep them in good order, and when living rooms are warmed up, the air is capable of holding much more water vapour. It becomes uncomfortably dry for plants as moisture from their leaves is attracted out of them into the surrounding atmosphere in excessive amounts, causing several problems – browning and shrivelling leaf tips and edges, leaf and bud drop, yellowing and wilting, for example. Unfortunately, this can also be a sign of incorrect watering, over-feeding or under-potting. It is somewhat of a sad joke with gardening pundits that whenever they are consulted about houseplants looking sick there could be a standard answer – air too damp, air too dry; too much water, not enough water; too hot, too cold; too little food, too much food; too little light, too much light; too big a pot, too small a pot! It is only when you have the chance of actually viewing the 'body' that you can get a real picture of what has gone wrong.

I have already touched on the ways that an excessively dry atmosphere can be improved as far as houseplants are concerned. The most practical way is to group them together so the combined moisture given off by them raises the humidity and helps each plant to help its neighbours. Standing the pot, or pots, in a larger outer container of moist peat, bark, perlite, vermiculite, sand, Hortag or pebbles will also make the air moister but, as I have stressed already, the inner pot base must not be standing in water. Misting the leaves once or twice a day with a hand sprayer containing warm water is

Houseplants *(previous page)* grouped together will often grow more happily than as isolated specimens

Joseph's coat (croton) *(top left)* and *Cordyline terminalis (top right)* will tolerate some direct sunshine

Begonia semperflorens (below) will flower for many months in a light spot with some sun

helpful, but do take care not to damage furnishings. Do not mist in bright sunlight or you could cause the leaves to scorch, and it is better not to mist late in the day if the night temperature in the room drops more than a few degrees or it can encourage diseases. Misting also helps to cool down the plant when the room is very warm, and it discourages red spider mite which can be a problem in an over-dry atmosphere.

Very occasionally, not usually in the home but sometimes in a conservatory or other glass structure, there can be too much humidity. This is the commonest cause of the failure of plants in bottle gardens, the terrarium, and other confined glass containers. Botrytis, a form of grey mould, sets in, patches of rot appear on the stems and leaves, any flowers turn mouldy and, in bad cases, the whole plant can collapse. Sometimes the trapped air around a tightly massed group of plants can become over-saturated with moisture; being stagnant, problems can occur here, too. The best way to deal with over-humidity is to increase the ventilation so the plant can receive more fresh air. Where plants in a group develop problems through over-humid conditions, thinning them out slightly or moving the individual pots away from each other somewhat will help. Grey mould can be controlled to some extent by spraying with a fungicide such as benomyl, but the best remedy is to improve the growing conditions.

Fresh air has other benefits. It helps to lower the temperature when it has become uncomfortably high, it can strengthen plant tissue and increase disease resistance, and it also helps to lower the concentration of any toxic fumes (toxic as far as plants are concerned, that is), like those emitted from some inefficient solid fuel burning stoves. Many plants, though not those which originated from the steamier parts of the tropics, will tolerate, and often enjoy, a spell outside in a warm, sheltered position during the height of summer.

Fresh air should not be confused with draughts, and a sudden drop in temperature is also to be avoided. Do pick your times carefully in winter when you open the window; you will not be very popular with your houseplants if you subject them to an icy gale! Plants that have been in a draught or otherwise chilled will soon show signs of stress – sudden leaf dropping or yellowing is a characteristic symptom.

Hygiene
To ensure that houseplants are not subjected to unnecessary risks, it is essential to observe fairly strict rules of hygiene. For example, all flower

pots should be thoroughly washed before they are used again for repotting as pests and diseases can easily be transferred from one plant to another this way. Saucers and outer containers should also be regularly washed, and a periodic wipe down of the plant pot itself does not come amiss.

In addition, the plants themselves should be regularly cleaned to prevent a build-up of dust, which is harmful as it blocks the breathing pores. It is not always realized that a heavy build-up of dust can exclude enough daylight to affect the plant's ability to function properly, and besides, dusty plants look terrible! Removing dust can be done in several ways. Where feasible the best method is to submerge the whole plant in a bucket of water, but do not do this with hairy leaved plants, as the water trapped among the hairs can often cause the leaves to rot. If this is not practical, the leaves should be thoroughly syringed with warm water until all the dirt runs off them. Plants with larger leaves can be sponged individually. Spiny and hairy plants should be dusted by brushing lightly with a very soft brush.

Larger leaved and leathery plants are improved in appearance once they have been cleaned by giving them a shine. You have to be careful which plants you do this to, as there are certain ones which are not suitable, generally those with very soft or hairy leaves, and some of fairly primitive constitution, like ferns and, in some cases, palms. The product you choose will have a list on the label of plants you should avoid trying to shine up.

Leaf shine preparations come in several forms. The best known is that made by Bio, which is applied as a milky liquid with a piece of cotton wool or small portion of sponge, and left to dry on to a shine. There are also aerosols, which are effective, but the plant must be sprayed well away from anything which you do not want the liquid to fall on. There are also ready-impregnated sponges and tissues, some of which have plant foods or an insecticide incorporated. Do not be tempted to put into practice some of the traditional suggestions for shining leaves – using milk will not make them shine and smells awful after a while; beer and vinegar have more of a cleaning effect than a polishing one, and olive oil, while producing some sort of sheen, encourages dust to stick to the leaves and very soon clogs the pores.

Pests

Even if you give your houseplants the best attention in the world, you sometimes cannot avoid them contracting pests and diseases. With a few exceptions, most are not serious if attended to in time, but if treatment is neglected, eventually the plants can become seriously affected. The following are the most common problems, their symptoms, and the remedy required.

Aphids are small, usually green, insects which cluster on the tender young shoots and leaves. They suck the sap and weaken and distort the shoots. The plant should be sprayed with an insecticide which is recommended for houseplants such as Bio 'Sprayday' or Boots' Houseplant Insecticide.

Caterpillars are not often found on plants in the home, but can be a pest of those in the conservatory where butterflies and moths have been able to enter to lay their eggs. Hand picking is the best remedy.

Earwigs can disfigure houseplants by making holes in the leaves and eating the flowers. If you suspect infestation with earwigs, they can generally be dislodged by shaking the plants and squashed. It is better to turn to chemical methods of controlling pests only as a last resort in the confines of the home.

Fungus gnats appear usually as small, black, winged insects which fly around the surface of the compost. They do no harm in themselves but lay eggs on the compost which hatch into small, white black-headed maggots which, though usually also harmless in that their staple diet is decaying organic matter, can sometimes vary the menu and eat young roots. Fungus gnats tend to favour over-wet conditions, and can be controlled by cutting down on the watering and drenching the compost with malathion.

Mealy bug looks like white cotton wool clinging to the stems of houseplants, but this is in fact a cluster of small sap-sucking insects covered with white fluff. This fluffy coating is waterproof, so the pests are difficult to control; the best method of dealing with them is to wipe them off, using a cotton bud moistened with surgical spirit.

Red spider mite is a tiny sap-sucking creature related to the spider. It is particularly widespread among houseplants grown in hot, dry air. Symptoms are a mottling and blotching of the upper surface of the leaves. The mites themselves can be found on the undersides, which feel 'gritty' to the touch and are sometimes strung with white webbing. Although a houseplant insecticide gives some measure of control, there is no really effective remedy for red spider mite other than misting the leaves at least once a day to create moister conditions and, where possible, increasing the humidity in the vicinity of the infested plants.

Scale insects look rather like miniature brown barnacles stuck to the stems of plants; like mealy bug, they are waterproof, so are best removed with a damp cloth or cotton bud. Watering the soil with a systemic insecticide such as dimethoate is sometimes effective, and spraying with a houseplant insecticide after removing the pests will help to prevent their return – for a while, at any rate.

Springtails are wingless, dirty white, grey or brown jumping insects. Like fungus gnat grubs, they usually feed on decaying vegetable matter, but occasionally develop a taste for live roots. Treatment is the same as for fungus gnats.

Symphylids are related to millipedes. They are small, brown and active and have twelve pairs of legs. They are like fungus gnats in that they generally eat dead plant matter but can sometimes turn their attention to living material. Control is similar to that for fungus gnats and springtails. Roots being damaged by these pests will eventually cease to function properly and in a bad attack the plant leaves turn yellow and start to wilt.

Thrips, or thunder flies, are those irritating tiny black insects which sometimes appear in their millions in hot, humid weather. They are not a serious pest of houseplants but can damage begonias and fuchsias, causing a silvery streaking of the leaves and distorted flowers. The plants should be sprayed when necessary with a houseplant insecticide.

Vine weevils are perhaps the most dreaded of all pot plant pests. The adult is not the real culprit, although it does eat the edges of the leaves; it is the fat, white, creamy grub which does the damage with its voracious appetite for roots, especially those of the polyanthus and fuchsia. You will usually find dozens of the little beasts in an affected pot. Sometimes the houseplant begins to look yellow and unhealthy, but usually the first sign of infestation is when the whole thing collapses. Turn it out of its pot and you will find a collection of revolting grubs and virtually no roots.

Control is difficult – in the home you don't usually notice the adults. In the greenhouse they can sometimes be trapped in corrugated paper or sacking overnight, which is then burnt as soon as possible. Lindane, otherwise known as BHC or gamma-HCH, is about the only soil insecticide which has any effect at all on the grubs. It is persistent and highly toxic and there is a great deal of pressure being brought to bear to have it banned, as far as the amateur market is concerned, at least. Incorporating lindane into the soil at potting time will ensure the plants are kept free from vine weevil grubs for up to three months, but watering with the same chemical is the only subsequent control.

Whitefly is another troublesome indoor pest. This is a tiny white moth-like creature, and again, it is the greenish larvae which congregate on the undersides of the leaves which cause the trouble, as they suck the sap and, like aphids and scale insects, leave a sticky deposit of honeydew. A bad infestation can cause leaves to turn yellow and drop. Plants should be sprayed with a houseplant insecticide containing permethrin; because of the life cycle of the insect this should be repeated every three days until there are no more signs.

Diseases

Anthracnose is a fungus causing sunken black spots on the leaves of certain susceptible species. Dark brown streaks may also appear at the tips of the leaves, and the disease is made worse by warm, moist conditions. Improving the ventilation, preventing overcrowding, and spraying with a fungicide will help to control the disease. Affected leaves should be removed and burnt.

Botrytis (grey mould) has already been described on page 33. It is a disease of damp, humid, badly ventilated conditions, so if the environment is improved the disease should disappear. All affected plant tissue should be removed and burnt, and what remains sprayed with a fungicide. Watering and misting must be reduced until the plant recovers. Immediate action is essential or an attack can prove fatal.

Crown and stem rot looks like its name, a rotting of the stem base or the crown of the plant. It is caused by a fungus and is usually fatal – pot, compost and dead plant should be disposed of hygienically (*not* on the compost heap). Overwatering, cool conditions and poor ventilation are the usual causes.

Leaf spots are caused by both fungi and bacteria and appear as sunken brown areas on the leaves of susceptible plants. These spots can merge to kill the whole leaf. Affected leaves should be picked off and burned and the plant sprayed with a fungicide. The disease is usually worse in moist conditions, so increasing the ventilation and keeping the plant on the dry side for a few weeks can help.

Powdery mildew is a fungal disease which appears as a white powdery coating. It is not fatal, but looks unsightly and can disfigure both the leaves and any flowers. Badly affected leaves should be removed and the plant sprayed with a fungicide.

Root rot is a serious disease which is usually caused by overwatering. Badly affected plants nearly always die, less seriously damaged ones can have remedial treatment as described on page 22. If a lot of your plants are succumbing to this disease, there is something wrong with your watering technique.

Sooty mould is a secondary fungal infection growing on the sticky honeydew secreted by whitefly, aphids, mealy bug and scale insects. Removing the pests will help; the mould itself can be cleaned off by wiping the leaves with warm water. If this is not done it can clog the pores of the plant and affect its breathing.

Virus is not a common disease, but sometimes appears as a distorting of the stems or leaves, or a yellowing or mottling of the leaves for which there is no other obvious reason. Plants bought from reliable sources are seldom affected; it is more often found in cuttings passed around from one person to another. There is no cause, and plants suspected of having a virus disease should be discarded.

Houseplants and holidays

I knew an old lady once who had not had a holiday for forty years because she was afraid to leave her massive collection of houseplants to the tender mercies of anyone else! While I sympathize with her, there are certain steps you can take to make sure you get at least an annual break.

Of course, the reliable neighbour is the best bet. If you can, pick the one who has the greatest success with houseplants himself or herself; if not, try to spend some time with them before leaving to show them just what you mean by 'watering' – that is, when the plants need it, not a weekly drowning or a daily dribble. It is just as upsetting for the person who has been entrusted with your precious plants to find them dying under their very nose as it is for you to come home and find a heap of lifeless compost-heap fodder.

To help the person who is going to 'baby sit' for you, wherever practical all your houseplants should be collected together into one place, preferably one which is light but not sunny. This saves your friend having to go in search of them and avoids the risk of some of them being missed out. This is more important in summer than in winter as the plants will need more frequent watering. Unless you are going away for a very long period in winter, you may even find that you can move all your plants into a place with a temperature of about 50°F (10°C) and good natural daylight and they won't need any attention until you get home – the rest will do them good!

If you have no one to whom you can entrust this task, there are other ways of ensuring your houseplants get sufficient water. Again, this mainly applies to summer absences. One method is to place capillary matting under your plants (on a tray with sides capable of containing water). This matting can either be left very damp or, if you intend to be away a long time, it can be kept moist by making a strip of it into a wick – one end is placed under the main piece of capillary matting to keep it in place, and the other is submerged in a reservoir of water. The matting should keep moist through capillary action as long as the wick is touching water in the reservoir. This method may again mean having to mass all your plants together in order to utilize the matting fully.

There are some excellent drip-feed watering devices available now. They are more suitable for the conservatory than the home, however, and are connected to the mains tap; water drips slowly into the compost through a series of narrow plastic tubes to keep the compost moist.

If you have to go away in a hurry and have no capillary matting to hand, you can make a temporary substitute out of damp newspaper. Depending on how many plants are in question, these are stood in the bottom of a sink or bath (in natural light, of course) and the cold tap left to drip onto them. Capillary action will again keep them moist, if not as efficiently as in the case of specially designed capillary matting. Be warned, however – the newsprint can sometimes stain the surface of the bath (in rare cases, permanently!) and you may get a ring of lime scale on the bath sides around the top of the newspaper, though this will usually come off by rubbing it with neat vinegar.

Capillary matting will not work if pebbles or crocks have been used to assist drainage in the flower pots as the capillary action will be broken. There is no need to 'crock' plant pots these days if peat-based compost and containers with adequate drainage holes are used.

If you only have the odd plant, moisture can be conserved for a short time by sealing it in a clear polythene bag. Do not leave it in the sun, or the contents will cook!

Houseplants capable of standing cooler conditions can even be put outside in a sheltered place to advantage. This method of keeping them happy is especially useful if you have a neighbour coming to water outdoor plants for you, as the whole lot can be dealt with together.

The conservatory owner is well advised to think about an automatic watering system anyway, not just for the holiday period, as plants in conservatories, unless they are on the shady side of the house, tend to need more watering. You may have to revert to watering manually in winter, though, to avoid too much being given.

All the care and attention you can lavish on a plant will not help it, though, if it is expected to grow in a place it is not suited for. In the next sections of this book I shall attempt to identify the different areas where plants are likely to be required, and give my recommendations for those that should grow without too much trouble in these particular locations.

Plants for specific regions in the home

Positions in full sun

Positions receiving full sunlight are likely to be windowsills facing south, south-west or south-east, south-facing conservatories (these will usually have some shading or conditions can become intolerable), and the floor area directly inside a south-facing patio door or French window. The sun is very hot in this position, and many plants are likely to be harmed unless some screening is provided. Often a well-gathered, good quality net curtain is sufficient to reduce glare to a more tolerable level, enabling a wider range of plants to be grown, but the air temperature can also get very high on fine days, and plenty of ventilation should be given. The following plants are ones which should thrive in direct sunlight, though on really sweltering days they may show some signs of distress and should be moved back from the window slightly.

Cacti and succulents are an obvious choice. Their specially modified swollen leaves and stems, often with hairs and spines to cut down transpiration, are capable of dealing with drought and heat. Cacti usually come from desert regions of the world and therefore are well used to soaring temperatures by day and plummeting ones by night. Succulents originate from many parts of the globe, but they, too, are adapted to cope with high temperatures and water in short supply. There are so many varieties of both that it would be impossible to give a comprehensive list in a book of this nature, so I can only single out a few for special mention.

Opuntias are the cacti we usually think of as one of the main features of Western films. They have characteristically flat, segmented stems and are quite often, though not always, very spiny. They are not as free-flowering as some of the 'barrel' types of cactus. **Mammillarias** are perhaps the most free-flowering of those widely available to the amateur gardener, though some forms of **echinocactus**, **echinocereus**, **hamatocactus**, **lobivia**, **parodia** and **rebutia** also flower well. Cacti in the home look best if displayed in shallow pans in collections of several different forms, alternatively a spectacular effect can be achieved if a whole section of a sunny conservatory is given over to them.

Succulents, on the other hand, are often more conventional in form and many display well as isolated specimens. Most are very easily propagated just by breaking off pieces and planting them in a free-draining compost, and so succulents are widely exchanged between gardening friends. One of the most popular is ***Crassula argentea***, otherwise known as the money plant, jade plant or friendship plant, which, when growing well, is a multi-branched plant with a thick trunk and branches, and fleshy round leaves.

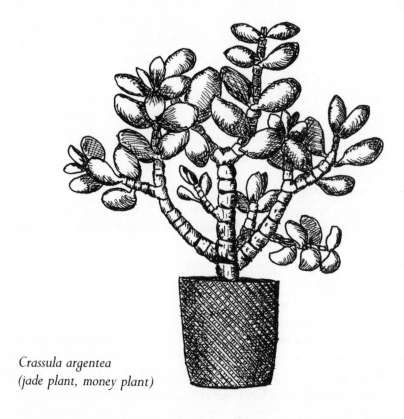

Crassula argentea
(jade plant, money plant)

Other succulents commonly encountered are the **agaves**, which produce stiff, narrow leaves, often with spines at the tips or sharp serrated edges, from a central rosette at ground level. Similar but smaller are the **aloes** and **haworthias**. Another rosette-forming succulent, resembling the houseleek but sometimes producing rosettes on the end of stiff stems, is **echeveria**; **aeonium** is not dissimilar. A plant popular with those who like to give and receive is ***Bryophyllum daigremonteanum***, which produces tiny, perfectly-formed plantlets all along its leaf edges which take root in the compost around the base when they drop off. A few succulents have a trailing habit and are eminently suitable for hanging pots in warm, sunny rooms. These are dealt with on page 88 and 89.

Whereas most cacti have spectacular flowers which are at least as important as their curious shapes, in general the inflorescences of succulents are not nearly so striking. Many succulents with branching habits benefit from being cut back or pinched out periodically to improve the shape.

A succulent which is usually bought as a temporary flowering houseplant is the **kalanchoë**. Some kalanchoës are grown for their leaf forms but one species, *Kalanchoë blossfeldiana*, sometimes called flaming Katy, produces attractive flower heads of red, orange, pink or yellow depending on the cultivar. Compact varieties are available like 'Tom Thumb' and 'Vesuvius'. The old favourite 'Vulcan' can be easily grown from seed. This plant is usually bought as a temporary splash of colour, but can be saved to flower another year. Its natural flowering period is in spring, but plants in flower can be purchased at almost any time of the year – the grower regulates the hours of daylight and darkness it receives to achieve this.

A point to bear in mind is that most commonly grown succulents are quite happy spending the summer on a warm patio or similar position outside.

The **Coleus** is easily propagated from seed or cuttings, which is why you often see it at bazaars and like functions. It is a highly colourful plant, with variegated, slightly nettle-shaped leaves (which has earned it its common name of flame nettle) in a most amazing range of colours and patterns. It is undemanding; all it requires is good light and regular pinching out of the growing tips to make it bushy. It has an insignificant blue flower spike, which is also best pinched out – this encourages new shoots to form instead.

Celosia is another family of temporary houseplants which are discarded after flowering, and are perhaps better known by their popular names. *Celosia plumosa*, the plume flower, has feathery plumes of red or yellow. *Celosia cristata*, or cockscomb, has a strangely shaped, convoluted flower head, also of red or yellow. They revel in full sun, but if the temperature gets too high the flower display is over more quickly, so adequate ventilation is desirable.

Capsicum annuum, the Christmas pepper, is another of those houseplants you more often receive as a gift than buy yourself. Most varieties have cone-like fruits which change as they mature from green through yellow to red, so all three colours can be on the plant at the same time. Although Christmas is one of the most popular times for them, you can also find capsicums around in the spring and summer. If the compost is always kept moist the fruits should last for several months, and can be used (very sparingly!) in cooking afterwards. If red spider mite becomes a problem, the plant should be misted daily and stood on a saucer of moist pebbles. Some treatment for aphids may also be necessary.

Irsine is a real sun-lover, as it becomes drawn up even in light shade. There are two common forms grown as houseplants: *Irsine herbstii*, the bloodleaf or beefsteak plant, which has dark red leaves with pink veins, and *I. herbstii* 'Aureoreticulata', which has red stems and green leaves with wide yellow veining. Irsine can be easily propagated from stem cuttings in late spring.

Relatives of capsicum are **Solanum capsicastrum** and **S. pseudocapsicastrum**, the winter cherry (the latter has larger berries). These have attractive orange or red berries on shrubby plants during winter, which follow small white flowers of a similar shape to the tomato and potato, to which it is also related. The berries are poisonous, so the plant should not be grown where there are small children about. If it is pruned back after fruiting then repotted and stood outside during summer, it should produce another crop of berries – these can be helped to set by misting the flowers with water. The plant is brought back into the house for the winter.

The popular zonal, regal and ivy-leaved **pelargoniums** are too well-known to need describing. Zonal pelargoniums are now easily raised from seed, although if you hve a favourite variety it must be propagated from cuttings. There is a wide colour range from pure white to purple. Ivy-leaved 'geraniums' as they are commonly (and incorrectly) referred to, are useful hanging-basket plants for a hot, sunny room (see page 88). Zonal pelargoniums will flower nearly all the year round if they receive enough sun, though they will have to be cut back occasionally to prevent them getting too 'leggy'. Regal pelargoniums, which are propagated from cuttings in late summer, have bigger and more spectacular flowers, but the season is not as long.

The shrimp plant, **Beleperone guttata**, is an interesting plant with salmon-coloured flower heads which vaguely resemble large prawns, hence its common name. It is an undemanding plant, provided it receives plenty of sun and cool nights, and is cut back annually to make a bushy specimen.

The pineapple plant, **Ananas comosus**, and its variegated form, **A. comosus 'Variegatus'**, are bromeliads. Bromeliads originate in the American jungle, and are usually epiphytes – that is, they use other plants for anchorage but not for food, so are not parasites. They therefore need to obtain their food through other methods than by absorption through the roots, which are only used for holding on with. Most bromeliads collect water in the central rosette of stiff, strap-like leaves they generally have; in the wild, dead matter falls into this which feeds the plants, but when growing as houseplants, very dilute liquid feed is added to the water which is poured into the centre of the rosette, or 'vase' which some bromeliads have. Because most come from forest regions, they prefer to be shaded from direct hot sun, but the pineapple plants seem to revel in it. Occasionally, small pineapples will be produced from the centre of the leaves, which are fringed with nasty, jagged serrations, so care must be taken when handling them.

A plant which will stand quite a lot of bright light and warmth is the trailing **senecio**, Senecio macroglossus. It has a variegated form, S. macroglossus 'Variegatus', and a relative with an interestingly-shaped green leaf, S. mikanioides. The common names of Cape Ivy and German Ivy respectively are highly descriptive – until you examine them carefully you could be fooled into thinking that they really are ivies, and yet they are no relation. With their succulent, waxy leaves, however, they are a far cry from the grey senecio that is such a common garden plant. They make very useful substitutes for ivy where conditions are too hot for ivies to be happy.

Sansevieria, or mother-in-law's tongue, will grow almost any-where, providing it is not overwatered, which is about the only way you can kill it. The true mother-in-law's tongue is Sansevieria trifasciata 'Laurentii', which has green, spiky, upright leaves banded with a lighter green and edged with gold. S. trifasciata is similar, but without the gold, and is usually referred to as the snake plant. There are also less commonly seen rosette-forming types such as S. 'Hahnii' and S. 'Hahnii

Sansevieria trifasciata 'Laurentii'
   (mother-in-law's tongue)

Gold'. It is interesting to note that, although new plants can be formed by cutting a leaf into pieces and inserting them into compost, the resulting plants will lack their gold edges. The only way to propagate mother-in-law's tongue and ensure the gold edge remains is to divide a large plant into smaller sections and pot these up individually.

Yucca elephantipes, the spineless yucca, seems to raise more questions about its well-being than any other houseplant. There appear to be two kinds of people – those who can't grow it at all, and those

46

who grow it too well! The indoor yucca, although related to those grown outside, needs a warm situation and plenty of light to succeed; without these the rosettes of long pointed leaves will yellow and die, and the trunk of mature specimens will start to rot. The yucca can outgrow the average living room, but the thick, woody trunk can be cut back and new clumps of leaves will start to emerge lower down. Severed trunks can be cut into pieces and repotted – these will sometimes, though not always, produce roots and form new plants (see Ti-tree, page 121). Individual rosettes of leaves may also grow to form new plants if removed carefully and potted up, but need a 'bottom heat' (the temperature of the compost), of no less than 70°F (21°C).

Areas with some direct sunlight

Parts of a room which are likely to receive some direct sunshine, though not during the middle of the day when the sun is at its strongest, are east- and west-facing windowsills and those areas closest to them where the window is large enough to make an impact, and in the vicinity of an east- or west-facing patio door or French window. East- and west-facing conservatories also come into this section. The light in conservatories will be much brighter as there is usually glass on at least three sides and often forming the roof as well, so some shading will also be required here (an east- or west-facing conservatory generally has a south-facing side as well, even if this is shorter).

Begonias are useful plants for this kind of situation. Although it is too bright for some forms, those producing flowers prefer a good light. They are broadly divided into two categories: ones with large flowers and ones with attractive foliage.

Tuberous begonias are those which produce large, mainly double, spectacular blooms in a wide range of colours. They are generally raised by planting the dormant tubers (hollow side up) in trays of peat or individual pots of peat-based compost in spring, though they can be propagated from seed. Those started off in trays can be replanted in baskets or pots when the shoots are an inch (2.5 cm) or so high. As they grow larger, it is possible the plants will need potting on again – usually a 7–8-inch (18–20-cm) pot is the final size needed. They will start to flower around midsummer and continue until late autumn. At this point water is withheld, the tops will die back and can be picked off, and the tubers are stored in peat in a cool place until the following season.

Lorraine begonias are also good flowering houseplants – they have fibrous roots and a profusion of smaller flowers around Christmas. An improvement on these are the hiemalis hybrids which are similar, though with slightly larger flowers which are produced nearly all the year round. These last two types require cutting back – the lorraines after flowering, the hiemalis types when they begin to look straggly.

The second type of begonia which is suitable for this position is that which is grown primarily as a foliage plant, but with the bonus of flowers – more delicate than those just described, but nevertheless attractive in their own right. This type of begonia can also be sub-divided into groups. The cane-stemmed begonias grow several feet tall if not pruned, but they can be cut back annually in spring to promote bushiness. They need to be planted in a heavy container, and preferably a soil-based compost (John Innes No. 1 is best) to give the plants stability. The most widely found are the angel wing begonia, *Begonia coccinea*, which has wing-shaped leaves with red undersides and red, pendant flowers; *B. lucerna*, sometimes called the spotted angel wing begonia, which has similarly-shaped though thinner leaves with a wavy margin and white spots, and clusters of pink flowers; and the trout begonia, *B. argenteo-guttata*, which has a glossy leaf, also spotted, similar flowers to *B. lucerna*, but a more bushy habit. Trailing begonias, for example, *B. glaucophylla*, the shrimp begonia, resemble the cane-stemmed forms in leaf and flower shape, but have a trailing habit. The flowers of *B. glaucophylla* are shrimp-pink in colour.

Mid-way between the very striking former group and the more subtle latter one are those begonias which form a bushy plant with both

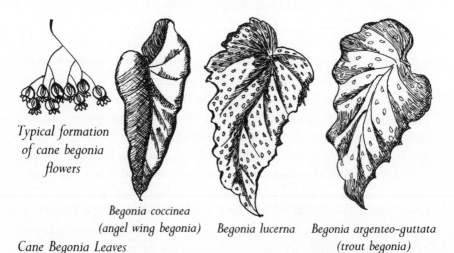

Typical formation of cane begonia flowers

Begonia coccinea (angel wing begonia)

Begonia lucerna

Begonia argenteo-guttata (trout begonia)

Cane Begonia Leaves

The umbrella tree *(top left)* tolerates a wide range of situations
Contrast leaf texture and colour for effective grouping *(top right)*
The sago palm *(below)* grows best in light shade

Air plants (tillandsias) need the minimum amount of watering *(left)*
Primulas make good flowering plants for light, unheated rooms
Aechmea (urn plant) will take central heating in its stride *(overleaf)*

interesting leaves and flowers. Among these are the popular *Begonia semperflorens*, which is usually encountered as a bedding plant but makes an excellent houseplant, with shiny leaves ranging from bright green to purple and a continual profusion of pink, white or red flowers; *B. fuchsioides*, the fuchsia begonia, which has glossy, serrated leaves and large, pendant, fuchsia-like flowers; *B. haageana*, the elephant ear begonia, with large, hairy leaves with red undersides and pale pink flowers; and *B. serratipetala*, the pink spot begonia, which has green serrated leaves blotched with red and deep pink flowers. All this category strike very easily from cuttings, and are more often obtained as plants passed from hand to hand than they are as specimens to buy from the garden centre.

I have already mentioned that most cacti and succulents thrive in full sun, but there are certain forms which originated in sub-tropical forests and jungles. These **forest cacti** still need some sun, but should be shaded from the really searing midday rays, so do well in the kind of position we are looking at. The two most popular are the Christmas cactus, **Schlumbergera truncata**, and its hybrids, which produce flowers in various shades of pink, and the Easter cactus, **Rhipsalidopsis gaertneri**, which also has several hybrid forms and

Rhipsalidopsis gaertneri
(Easter cactus)

similar flowers to the Christmas cactus, though usually red and later in the year (not always at Easter, unfortunately!). **Epiphyllum ackermanii**, the orchid cactus, is a related species; this has stems with notches in it and huge, exotic blooms, usually red, in late spring. There is another common forest cactus, **Aprocactus flagilliformis**, otherwise known as the rat's tail cactus; this has round green stems with soft prickles and flowers rather like the Christmas cactus.

To ensure a display of flowers every year, it pays to rest forest cacti for a few months after flowering by keeping them cool and dry. This can be achieved by moving them outside for the summer into a spot which is shaded from midday sun. They are brought inside again in the autumn. It is a good idea not to move the plants while the flower buds are forming, as they can sometimes drop off.

The **pot chrysanthemum** is a favourite plant for presents, and modern varieties are certainly very attractive, with lots of blooms in many colours. They need sunlight, providing it is not too hot, for all the flower buds to open, but high air temperatures can cause the flowers to die prematurely. Pot chrysanthemums can usually be purchased at any time of the year and are brought into flower by the nurseryman by giving a regulated amount of light and darkness. They have also been treated with a growth retardant, so although they can be planted in the garden and will often survive to flower quite happily there in subsequent autumns, the plants will be considerably taller than they were when you bought them.

The **Codiaeum (croton)**, or Joseph's coat, is more difficult to grow well than many of my recommendations, though in this position there should be no trouble. *Codiaeum variegatum* 'Pictum' is the form with large multi-coloured leaves and is the most temperamental; those with thinner leaves variegated green and white, like *C. craigii*, are easier. Leaves will drop off if the plant is subjected to draughts, the humidity is too low, or the compost has been allowed to dry out; if your plant becomes leggy, improve the growing conditions, cut the stem back, and often several shoots will start to grow from lower down.

Cordyline terminalis and its various cultivars is closely related to the more common dracaena but requires more light. *C. terminalis* is also known as the flaming dragon tree because of its striking leaves flushed with red – the variety 'Tricolor' is variegated with yellow as well.

Although **dracaenas** will tolerate some shade, those with variegated leaves like *Dracaena marginata* 'Tricolor', *D. fragrans massangeana*, *D. fragrans lindenii*, *D. deremensis* 'Bausei', 'Warneckii', 'Rhoersii' and 'Janet Craig', *D. sanderiana* and *D. godseffiana* all need some sun for the markings to develop properly. An east-facing sunny spot is ideal as west sun can sometimes cause scorching of the cream sections of the leaf.

Apart from the yucca, there are few subjects which come up more in gardening question and answer sessions than the rubber plant, *Ficus elastica* **'Decora'**. Usually it is because all the leaves have dropped off, which in turn generally is because, being a rather 'architectural' plant, it is expected to grow in situations it does not like at all – dark, too hot or cold, airless or draughty. What it really likes is some sunshine, and a regular wiping of the leaves to prevent dust clogging the pores. There are some excellent coloured-leaved forms like 'Black Prince', 'Tricolor' and 'Doescheri' – these certainly won't thrive in dark places. The fiddle-leaf fig, *Ficus lyrata*, is a similar plant, though the leaves are wavy-edged and less leathery.

Rubber plants which have grown too tall can be cut back and will become branched trees; what has been removed can be cut into small sections containing a leaf and leaf axil. If the leaf is rolled up and tied with soft string to prevent excessive moisture loss and the cutting is inserted into a warm, damp compost with the leaf axil just below the surface, you can sometimes get these sections to root and form new plants. Alternatively, they can be 'air-layered' by partially severing the stem where the top is to be removed, covering the wound with damp peat and polythene, and waiting a few months until new roots have formed in the peat, when the top half of the plant can be detached completely and potted up.

Fuchsias are quite easy to grow indoors, but not so easy to re-establish in the home when they have been grown in a cool greenhouse, as they do not like the hot, stuffy environment, and must receive enough bright light to flower properly. The most successful way to grow a fuchsia indoors is to start with it as a very small plant or rooted cutting, which can then acclimatize itself to your conditions. Rooted cuttings should be pinched out a couple of times to encourage bushiness. If the flower buds or leaves start to fall, the ventilation should be increased and the temperature lowered if possible. Fuchsias should not be allowed to dry out, as this can also cause premature flower drop.

Busy lizzies (impatiens) are another old-time favourite; they strike easily as cuttings, even in water, and will flower practically non-stop if given enough light. Older varieties can sometimes get very tall and leggy; regular pinching-out will help to prevent this. The recently introduced strain known as 'New Guinea Hybrids' are particularly attractive; they have a bushy habit and a bonus of variegated leaves.

Busy lizzies need a lot of water and will soon droop if they become too dry, but occasionally a phenomenon called 'guttation' takes place, when little droplets appear around the leaf edges. It is caused by more water being taken up by the plant than can be lost through transpiration, and is a sign the air is rather on the humid side; increased ventilation should remedy the problem. Busy lizzies are particularly prone to red spider mite and aphids (see page 35).

We have already looked at **pelargoniums** (usually known as 'geraniums', although strictly speaking 'geranium' is an incorrect term) in connection with south-facing positions, but there is another group which appreciates the slightly cooler conditions of the east- or west-facing site. These are the ones grown for their ornamental, often scented, leaves, like the rose-scented geranium (*Pelargonium capitatum*), the lemon-scented geranium (*P. crispum*) and its variegated form, the peppermint geranium (*P. tomentosum*), the apple-scented geranium (*P. odoratissimum*), and another one which smells vaguely of roses when the leaves are crushed, *P. graveolens*, which, with its intricate and well-known leaf form, is perhaps the most easily recognized of all. Generally, scented-leaved geraniums are more often obtained as cuttings from people who have them already, although some of the smaller, family-run houseplant nurseries sometimes have them for sale. They are easily propagated from cuttings taken at more or less any time of the year.

The **hippeastrum** is more often referred to, again strictly speaking incorrectly, as the amaryllis. It is usually acquired as a large bulb around Christmas which has been specially treated to flower very soon after being potted up in a small half-pot of peat-based compost. A good bulb should have at least two flower spikes, and each head should have several large, trumpet-shaped florets. Colours range from pale pink to deep red. When the flower spike fades it should be removed at the base of the stem.

The plant should be kept indoors until summer, and watered and fed regularly. During the warmest months of the year it can be put outside in its pot in a sunny position to ripen the bulb. When autumn comes, watering and feeding should gradually cease; this will cause the leaves to die down. When they are brown and shrivelled, they are cut off, then the bulb is stored in its pot in a cool, dark, frost-free place until about February, when it is brought indoors into a sunny position, watering is recommenced and, with luck, you should get flowers in the spring. The hippeastrum should not be repotted for several years;

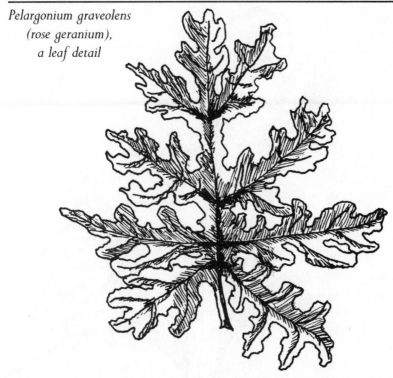

Pelargonium graveolens (rose geranium), a leaf detail

eventually it will produce young bulbs which can be removed once the plant is repotted, and planted up individually. If you do not remove the dead heads, seed will form and this can also be grown on into new plants – they will not come true to type and it will be several years before they flower, but it is an interesting experiment. It is advisable to keep young plants raised from seed growing continuously until they produce their first flower spike.

The **poinsettia (*Euphorbia pulcherrima*)** is yet another favourite gift plant around Christmas and is widely known as a bushy plant with white, pink or red bracts. To ascertain whether a plant is young enough to give a long period of enjoyment, have a look at the centre of the rosette of bracts. Here you will find the insignificant true flowers; if they are still in bud your plant should last well; if they are turning brown and shrivelled, however, its ornamental life for that season is nearly over and it should be left alone.

Poinsettias are usually discarded after flowering; if you want to save yours for another year, cut the stems down when the bracts have fallen and continue to water, with dilute liquid feed added, when necessary. New growths will soon appear, which should be thinned to leave the

(Amaryllis)
Hippeastrum hybrida
'Apple Blossom'

strongest five or six. At the end of September the plant is given the treatment described on page 41 – if you find it difficult to exclude all light you can pop a black polythene bag over it to give a period of total darkness. It will probably produce red bracts around the new year, but as this would also have been treated with a growth retardant in the nursery, the plant the following season will be very much taller.

Orchids have an air of the exotic about them, but there are some available from houseplant nurseries which are quite easy to grow in the home, although they are not cheap. Again, it would be impossible to list all the species which are obtainable and give full cultural details as this could constitute a book in itself, so I will confine myself to generalities and recommend you to further reading.

The most commonly found orchids for home cultivation come from the genera **cattleya**, **cymbidium**, **odontoglossum**, **paphio-pedilum** and **vuylstekeara**. Generally speaking, orchids should have a day temperature of about 70°F (21°C) in summer and 60°F (16°C) in winter, with a differential between day and night temperature of about 10°F (5°C). They should receive approximately 10–15 hours of good light a day; natural light can be supplemented with good artificial light if necessary in winter. The compost should always be kept moist, and water should be tepid and soft. Repotting should only take place when the pot is full – not sooner than every three years. At repotting time the pseudobulbs at the base of the plant can be divided if required to make new individual plants, but do not place these in too-large pots. Special orchid compost should be used (see page 29). In the wild, orchids do not receive a lot of nourishment and so the feed given during the summer months should be weak, or of a special kind developed for orchids. They like humid conditions, so daily misting is needed if the room atmosphere is very dry.

The **African violet (saintpaulia)** is another plant which seems to worry many people, and yet it is really quite easy to grow. It must receive good light to flower, though hot midday sun makes the leaves pale and browns the petals. Overwatering is the usual cause of death as it causes rot to set in at the crown. The roots can become quite dry without the plant coming to any harm. When the flowers have faded they should be removed at the base by giving the stems a half-twist – leaving pieces of stem on the plant to die back is another cause of rotting. Sometimes the plants may be infected with mildew; this can be controlled by spraying with a fungicide but they must be stood somewhere airy (not draughty) to dry off, as this is another cause of the leaves rotting. Propagation is usually by leaf cuttings as described on page 8. When removing the leaf you must make sure no piece is left on the plant to die back. Cut the leaf off as near the crown as possible, using a very sharp, pointed knife or, alternatively, twist it off as previously described.

Saintpaulia seed is available and is not too difficult to germinate – the resultant plants are a real old assortment, but it is interesting to see what you get. Some African violet growers claim to separate their plants when they get very big, by dividing them in pieces through the crown, again using a sharp knife, but this method is fraught with danger as many of the new plants rot off where the incision was made. African violet plants should not be over-potted, and will grow happily for many years in the same small pot if they are fed regularly. Half-pots are more suitable than full plant pots as the roots are fairly shallow.

Similar in requirements to African violets are **Sinningia speciosa (gloxinia)** and **streptocarpus**. Gloxinia used to be a very difficult plant to grow at one time, but more accommodating hybrids have been produced in recent years, and research is also going on into both this plant and streptocarpus (the Cape primrose) to get specimens of tidier habit with more compact leaves more evenly distributed around the crown. Gloxinia is usually bought as a plant in bud in summer and should flower for two or three months; dormant tubers can also be obtained in spring. These are potted up in peat-based compost and grown on in a temperature of no less than 60°F (16°C). After flowering, feeding and watering is withheld and the tuber will dry off. It is then stored in a cool place over winter. It prefers an east-facing position as the sun can be too hot during the afternoon. The compost must be kept moist, and tepid water should be used. Gloxinia can also be grown from seed, or pieces of leaf will strike as cuttings. Browning leaves or flower buds which fail to open are a sign that the air is too dry; when this happens, stand the pot on a tray of moist pebbles to increase the humidity.

The cultivation and propagation of streptocarpus is similar to that of the African violet, although the flowers are more like the gloxinia in shape. Gloxinia flowers are large and trumpet-shaped; those of the streptocarpus are also trumpet-shaped but more dainty. Streptocarpus benefits from annual repotting – the plants can successfully be divided at this time to make new ones. There is also some very good streptocarpus seed available.

Recently, an eye-catching cross between streptocarpus and gloxinia has become available. This has characteristics of both plants but seems to be easier to grow than either. Streptogloxinia, as it is called, is likely to become a popular flowering houseplant of the future.

The bright area with no direct sun

These conditions are found in the few feet adjacent to a sunny window away from where direct sunshine can reach, and also on a north-facing windowsill or other window area which does not receive direct sun (for example, where a building or tree prevents the light from reaching the house). A north-facing conservatory can have similar conditions, but remember, some sun may be able to enter through the other sides.

Most of the plants described in the previous section will also grow perfectly well, and sometimes to advantage, in this sort of location; they are, however, capable of tolerating or enjoying higher light levels and that is why I included them there. The following plants do not appreciate strong sunshine, but do need a light area to grow in if they are to look at their best.

Aphelandra squarrosa (zebra plant) is an eye-catching plant with

Aphelandra squarrosa 'Louisae'
(zebra plant)

striking striped leaves. The best leaf markings are to be found in *A. squarrosa* 'Brockfield'; *A. squarrosa* 'Dania' has a more compact form. *A. squarrosa* 'Louisae' is the one most commonly sold. At certain times the zebra plant has the additional attraction of producing interesting yellow flower spikes which look rather like elongated, inverted pineapples; these usually last six weeks or so. It needs warmth at all times and may require moving to a brighter spot in winter. Watering should be with tepid soft water and daily misting in summer is usually necessary. Care must be taken not to overwater in winter.

Asparagus is often incorrectly thought of as a fern, though it is in fact a close relative of the delicious and much sought-after vegetable. The two varieties most commonly seen are *Asparagus plumosus*, which has dark green, upright, delicate-looking, feathery foliage, and *A. sprengeri*, which is more trailing and coarser-looking. Sometimes you will also see the plume asparagus, *A. meyeri*, for sale, which has close

Asparagus plumosus

plumes of feathery foliage. These three varieties are very adaptable as far as watering, light and temperature are concerned, but too little watering or too much sun cause the foliage, which looks like tiny pine needles, to drop. *A. sprengeri* looks well in hanging pots (see page 85).

In addition to the **begonias** mentioned on page 48, there are others with interesting leaves which need light but no sun. In fact, all but the large-flowered tuberous kinds will thrive in this position. *Begonia rex* is the most exciting as there are so many different varieties, with leaves variegated with just about every colour you can think of. *B. rex* is ideal to incorporate in an arrangement of plants, but is very prone to botrytis, so should not be too crowded. Other common forms of foliage begonias are *B. masoniana*, the iron cross begonia, with leaves which are crinkled like a savoy cabbage and have a dark cross in the centre, *B. bowerii*, the eyelash begonia, which has markings around the edge reminiscent of eyelashes, *B. metallica*, the metallic leaf begonia and *B.* 'Tiger'. *B.* 'Cleopatra', the maple leaf begonia, has a leaf shaped very much like a maple and tinted red, giving the plant the appearance of a maple turning colour in autumn.

The secret of growing ***Cyclamen persicum***, the florist's cyclamen, is to keep it cool – preferably not above 60°F (16°C) and less if possible. The ideal spot is a north-facing windowsill, where it should bloom for months on end. Overwatering, as is so often the case with houseplants, is usually why the plant collapses. Water should never be allowed to stand on the fleshy crown or it can cause the corm to rot. Yellowing leaves and spent flower stalks should be removed completely by twisting them off at the base, otherwise botrytis can be encouraged (see page 37). Cyclamen are very prone to a pest called cyclamen mite which distorts the leaves and flowers; at the first sign of infestation the plant should be sprayed thoroughly with a houseplant insecticide.

Cyclamen can be grown from seed, but greenhouse accommodation is really necessary. The corm can be saved for many years; there is evidence of some around which are over a hundred years old. The best way to treat a corm after flowering is to reduce feeding and watering until the leaves die, then place the pot on its side under the greenhouse staging or in a sheltered place outside for a month or two to allow the corm to rest. In July it can be repotted and watered and brought indoors. It will start to grow again and produce flowers in late autumn.

The correct name of **cineraria** is *Senecio cruentus*, though I doubt if many people would know it as such. It is an attractive flowering plant with large, vaguely heart-shaped, slightly rough leaves topped by large heads of daisy-like flowers in many colours. It requires cool, light but sunless conditions, should not be allowed to dry out, likes a periodic misting, and prefers tepid water. In the right situation I have known one to flower for about eight weeks in late winter and early spring, though this length of time is unusual. The plants are discarded after they have finished flowering.

Dieffenbachia, the dumb cane, is not the plant to have around the house if there are children as the sap is mildly poisonous and can cause a nasty swelling or rash if it gets in or around the mouth, hence the popular name. Its other common name, leopard lily, is descriptive of the variegated markings on the leaves. The most popular dieffenbachia is *Dieffenbachia amoena*; the more eye-catching ones are cultivars of *amoena picta*, such as 'Exotica', 'Superba' and 'Rudolph Roehrs'. Dieffenbachia does not like draughts or low light levels, so may need a lighter position in winter. It requires high humidity, so an outer container filled with damp material as described on page 32 is advisable. Care should be taken not to overwater in winter. It is an easy plant to propagate from; either cut the stem into short pieces and use them as cane cuttings, or root the top crown of leaves in a warm compost, or remove basal offshoots at the base and treat as cuttings. Annual repotting is usually necessary. A healthy dieffenbachia can sometimes reach 4–6 feet (1.2–1.8 m) in height.

Dizygotheca elegantissima is a close relative of the castor oil plant (aralia or fatsia), although not as tolerant of shade. It has fingered, serrated leaves which are sometimes nearly black in colour. It is rather exacting as to water requirements – too much and it will rot, too little and it drops all its finely-fingered leaf lobes. If it becomes 'leggy', it can be cut back hard and will usually grow again.

Ficus benjamina, the weeping fig, is an attractive, large houseplant with bushy stems turning woody and a semi-pendulous habit. Although a near relative of the rubber plant, the leaves are smaller, daintier, and of a slightly different shape. It will stand most conditions, but in deep shade, hot dry air, or if it becomes over-dry at the roots, it will drop its leaves, though new ones will usually grow again. There is a good variegated form, but this must have good light.

The reason why many people have trouble growing **ivies (hedera)** is because they tend to keep them too warm. Nearly all ivies are bone-hardy, even those which are less so only become damaged in severely cold weather. The secret of growing ivies indoors successfully is, therefore, to keep the temperature down as much as possible. They are not keen on really dry, centrally heated rooms, but can be helped by opening the window whenever possible and creating a humid atmosphere around them. This will ensure they do not put on unhealthy, spindly growth and the leaves do not turn brown and drop off.

There is a vast selection to choose from, with varying leaf shapes and a wide range of variegations, both gold and cream. Plain green ivies are also attractive if the plants are in good order, and will tolerate light shade as well as bright, sunless conditions. Ivies should be regularly repotted, sometimes twice a year if they are growing well, as being pot-bound can lead to the roots drying out unduly, which will also cause the leaves to turn brown and drop. Where plain green shoots appear on variegated ivies they should be removed at source to avoid them 'taking over' the plant.

Monstera deliciosa is the famous Swiss cheese plant; the large leaves have deeply cut edges and holes in them. The Swiss cheese plant is really a climber, and although young plants are bushy, they become elongated with age, even if there are several shoots, so eventually the plant will need support. A moss-covered pole is the best method of support until the plant gets too large, then it needs a trellis or permanent anchorage points in the wall. The moss pole is particularly beneficial as it can be kept damp by misting it or inserting a reservoir with small holes in the base on the top, which gradually trickles water down the pole. The leafless appendages produced from the stem are aerial roots – in the wild they help to support the plant and also absorb food where any is available. They should not be cut off, but can be pushed into the compost in the pot or inserted into the moss pole – if this is sprayed with dilute liquid fertilizer occasionally these roots will take this up and feed the plant.

The Swiss cheese plant is tolerant of most situations except very bright sunlight and deep shade; it will even stand dry, warm, centrally-heated rooms if watering is increased. If the plant develops brown edges to the leaves, the humidity should be increased. Young leaves seldom have slits and holes in them, and if older ones start to lose this characteristic it is because the light is not bright enough.

Without remedial treatment a healthy plant will normally get too large for most modern rooms; it can be cut well back and should shoot again further down. The severed stem can be made into cuttings in the same way as that from a pruned rubber plant (see page 51). Large plants should be potted in a loam-based compost to give stability. In a tall conservatory, *Monstera deliciosa* will eventually flower and produce edible fruits; in Victorian times many large houses would keep one primarily for fruit for the table.

Peperomia is a large family of plants, some small and bushy, others with larger leaves and a more upright habit, and yet more are trailing and make good hanging pot plants (see page 89). The most easily available are *Peperomia caperata* (small, crinkled leaves, variegated in one form), *P. hederaefolia* (similar leaves, but larger), *P. argyreia*, otherwise known as the watermelon plant or rugby football plant (deeply veined,

Peperonia magnoliaefolia

silvery-green leaves), and *P. magnoliaefolia*, or desert privet, which is larger, more upright and has privet-shaped, leathery leaves variegated yellowish-cream and white. Peperomias can be slightly temperamental until you understand their needs – careful watering, no sudden variation in temperature, no draughts, and a minimum temperature of about 55°F (13°C) in winter. Too much shade is also detrimental, and where insufficient natural light is available in winter, they respond well to supplementary fluorescent lighting, so are good plants for the kitchen if not too steamy. Peperomias require repotting very infrequently. Propagation is from stem cuttings in upright varieties and leaf cuttings in the smaller, bushy kinds. *P. caperata*, *P. hederaefolia* and *P. argyreia* produce curious, upright, snake-like white flowers in summer.

Philodendron is a large genus related to monstera and, like that plant, is capable of tolerating a great deal. Most people know one species well, *Philodendron scandens*, the sweetheart plant, an easily grown climber with shiny, heart-shaped leaves, but there are many other climbing forms, most of which produce aerial roots like monstera, and which should be trained in a similar fashion. Among those to look out for are 'Red Emerald', which has a red stem; *P. hastatum* (elephant's ear), a similar plant, but with a glossier leaf and lacking the red stem; the velvety, dark-leaved 'Black Gold;'; 'Burgundy', a similar form to *P. hastatum*, but with red-tinted new leaves; *P. panduraeforme* (fiddle leaf); *P. tuxia*, which has long, thick, spear-shaped leaves; and *P. elegans*, a finely toothed-leaved form.

The philodendron family also contains some very large, bushy

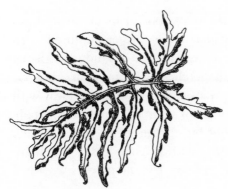

Philodendron selloum
(lacy tree philodendron)

Philodendron bipinnatifidum
(tree philodendron)

Leaves of Non-Climbing Philodendrons

63

varieties, which are often mistaken for monstera. The two most common are *P. bipinnatifidum*, the tree philodendron, and a form with very finely cut leaves with wavy edges, *P. selloum*, the lacy tree philodendron. These will need very large containers and a lot of space in time.

At the other end of the scale comes **pilea**, a genus of small bushy plants, and a few trailing ones (see page 89). The three most widely grown are *P. cadierei*, the aluminium plant, which has leaves marbled with silver; *P. involucrata*, the friendship plant – not to be confused with *Crassula argentea* on page 42 – the leaves of which are attractively patterned in silver and red; and *P.* 'Moon Valley', with green, crinkled leaves veined in red. Less widely seen are the red and white variegated *P.* 'Bronze'; the red-leaved *P. repens*, and an old favourite which is seldom offered for sale these days, *P. microphylla*, the artillary plant, which has very tiny leaves. Pileas require a great deal of water in summer but less in winter, and tepid water is beneficial. Old plants get straggly but can be persuaded to remain more bushy by pinching the tips out regularly. As new plants strike so well from cuttings, however, it is sometimes better to keep a regular supply of young plants and discard the older ones.

Scindapsus aureus, the Devil's ivy, and two other similar species, *S. aureus* 'Marble Queen' and *S. pictus*, are often thought to be variegated forms of *Philodendron scendens*, which, apart from the leaf colour, they resemble very much. They are not quite as easy to grow, however, as they do not tolerate such a wide range of temperatures, and they must be positioned in good light or the variegations will fade. They also require a fairly humid atmosphere.

Syngonium podophyllum, the goosefoot plant or arrow-head vine, is another climbing plant which tends to get confused with scindapsus, though it is easier to grow and the leaf is a different shape. As the plant gets older, the leaf shape changes from an arrow-head form until by the time the plant is mature it is a compound leaf with five lobes. Syngonium can be supported by tying to a cane or moss pole – older plants develop aerial roots but if the stems are cut back regularly the plant will remain bushy, with juvenile leaves which are very brightly coloured. If the roots get too dry, the oldest leaves will turn yellow and die.

Schefflera actinophylla, now re-named **Brassaia actinophylla**, the umbrella tree, and its smaller close relative, **Heptapleurum arboricola**, the parasol plant, make handsome specimens

Begonia rex (top) and Begonia 'Tiger' need a light position away from direct sun

Orchids such as this cymbidium *(top left)* require warmth, high humidity and
protection from strong sunshine
Dieffenbachia *(top right)* is a good foliage plant for a light but sunless place
The cineraria *(below)* needs a cool, light spot and plenty of water

Columnea gloriosa is a hanging plant for positions of high humidity *(previous page)*
A healthy basket of *Zebrina pendula (above)*
Saxifraga sarmentosa (below left) is an easy plant for a hanging pot
The variegated form of Swedish ivy *(below right)* is a cheerful and undemanding trailing plant

in a living room or hall. They will tolerate temperatures from 55–70°F (13–21°C) and light shade, but in darker conditions and higher temperatures tend to drop their leaf lobes. Schlefflera will get rather tall and lanky in time, but some of the long stems can be trimmed back. A variegated form of heptapleurum, *H. arboricola* 'Variegata', is becoming popular, especially in large mixed displays.

Indoor **vines** make excellent, though large, houseplants, and look good when trained around moss poles or onto free-standing trellis. The true vines are related to the grape vine, and most of the ones we grow indoors originated in Australasia and other far south areas of the southern hemisphere. The two most widely available are the shiny, toothed-leaved *Cissus antarctica*, or kangaroo vine, and *Rhoicissus rhomboidea* (grape ivy), which has a three-lobed compound leaf. There is an interesting newer variety around called *R. rhomboidea* 'Ellen Danica', with more deeply lobed compound leaves. More unusual vines are *Cissus discolor*, the begonia vine, which has a leaf rather like some of the foliage begonias with a red underside, and *Cissus striata*, which looks very much like Virginia creeper. *Rhoicissus capensis*, the Cape grape, is quite different, with large, unlobed leaves which are brown and furry

Cissus antarctica (kangaroo vine)

Rhoicissus rhomboidea (grape ivy)

Rhoicissus rhomboidea 'Ellen Danica' (mermaid vine)

Indoor Vines Leaf Details

on the underside. *Tetrastigma voinierianum*, the chestnut vine, also resembles Virginia creeper, and is a very rapid grower, so is only suitable for larger rooms and conservatories. It is a good hall plant as it likes to be kept cool – the other vines mentioned are fairly temperature tolerant but can drop their leaves if the air gets over-warm and too dry.

Spring bulbs have been used for many years as temporary indoor decoration. The most popular are hyacinths, daffodils and narcissi and tulips, but a wide range of other bulbs can be cultivated in pots, for example crocuses, snowdrops, scillas, grape hyacinths, chionodoxa and *Iris reticulata*. Spring bulbs can either be forced to flower in winter and early spring, or grown in containers in the garden for bringing into the house around the same time as they are in flower out of doors. Forced bulbs should be varieties which are suitable for this treatment and many bulbs will have been 'prepared', that is, given a special temperature treatment to encourage them to mature early. These bulbs are potted during the period August to October and around 12 weeks elapses before they are in flower. Specially designed bulb bowls are the usual containers, though ordinary plant pots and other receptacles can be used. Where the container has no holes in it, a special bulb fibre, similar to ordinary peat-based compost but with the addition of charcoal and oyster shell to keep it sweet, should be used.

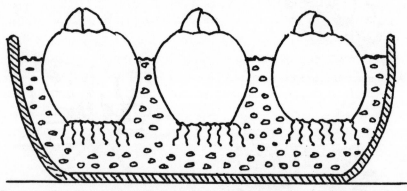

Diagram showing correct planting of prepared hyacinths in bulb bowl

To pot up bulbs for indoor forcing, first check them to make sure they are firm and healthy, with no soft or diseased patches on them. A layer of moist compost is then placed in the base of the container, enough for the tips of the bulbs to be above the surface when potting is complete and to allow about ½ inch (1 cm) between the top of the compost and the rim of the bowl. Place the bulbs on this layer – do not push them into the compost. The bulbs can be positioned quite close together but must not touch each other or the sides of the bowl, otherwise rotting can occur. The spaces between the bowl and the bulbs and the bulbs themselves are then filled with compost to the level described, and gently firmed with the fingertips. The completed bowls must then be given a period of complete darkness for around ten weeks to allow a good root system to develop. A cool position is essential – around 40°F (4.5°C). The best place for this is in a cold cupboard, or in a frost-free garage or shed, provided light is excluded.

The bowls are moved out of the dark when the shoots are between 1–2 inches (2.5–5 cm high). At this stage they should be placed in a cool, shady spot for a few days, but they can be moved into a lighter position later. A bright place without direct sunlight is ideal – sun tends to shorten the life of the flowers, especially if the room is warm. Some twiggy supports or canes and soft twine may be necessary to support the bulbs as they grow.

After flowering, you should continue to feed and water until the leaves start to yellow, when the bulbs can be removed from their containers, cleaned, and stored in the shed or garage until next autumn, when they can be planted in the garden. They will not be suitable for indoor cultivation again.

Bulbs grown in the garden for indoor decoration are potted up in the same way, but it is essential to use containers with drainage holes in the base as otherwise they will get waterlogged. The completed pots are placed close together in a sheltered place outside, and covered with straw or peat to break the frost. They are brought in when there is a good top growth, and treated in the same way as forced bulbs.

If this procedure is followed, you should have no problems. Those which do occur are because of some defect in cultivation. If you do not give a long enough period of darkness, it could stunt the growth, but too long encourages over-tall, limp growth. Keeping the bowl too warm during the period of darkness may cause stunted flowers, or even no flowers at all. Well-formed buds which fail to open are a sign of erratic watering – the compost should be kept damp, but not wet, at all times. Too wet compost will also cause the flowers to rot.

Do not be tempted to mix different types of bulbs and different varieties and colours in the same bowl – they will all flower at different times and not give a proper display. If you want to mix different sorts, they should be grown individually and made up into mixed bowls when nearly in flower; only then can you be reasonably sure that they will all flower at the same time.

The position in light shade

Light shade occurs in those parts of a room which are several feet away from a sunny window – south, east or west not shaded by plants or buildings – or in the immediate vicinity of a window or patio door which receives no sun at all. It should still be light enough for you to be able to do close work – knitting, sewing, drawing and the like – without having to resort to artificial illumination. Many of the plants suggested in the previous section would survive here, and if there is something among that list that you really feel you must have, but the position is somewhat shaded, it is worth a try. The most successful are likely to be asparagus fern, green-leaved ivies, *Ficus benjamina* (weeping fig), *Monstera deliciosa*, philodendron, schlefflera and non-variegated forms of heptapleurum. In addition, the following species are likely to succeed.

Aspidistra elatior, that favourite of Victorian parlours, is not as indestructible as its reputation suggests. It thrived in the living rooms of yesteryear because they were generally cooler and more humid than our centrally heated homes are today. In a very hot, stuffy environment the leaves develop brown tips, so the secret of success is to give the plant a cool, buoyant atmosphere. There is no need to repot more than every 5 or 6 years. The variegated form prefers a slightly warmer and lighter spot, but not in direct sunlight.

I have already mentioned **Bromeliads** on page 45. They are included in this section as well because, although they can tolerate lighter conditions and even some direct sunlight if not too strong, they will also do well in light shade.

Bromeliads for home decoration can be divided into two categories: those grown for their leaf coloration, and those with interesting flower spikes. Bromeliads really need no soil at all, as this is only for anchorage, and an interesting way of displaying them is to fix them, using a special adhesive which is obtainable at garden centres, to an attractively-shaped dead branch, secured in a container by means of stones and cement or plaster of paris. The most suitable for this purpose are those with a 'vase' as they are the easiest to water – the 'vase', of course, should be in an upright position so the water does not run out.

A similar idea which has become very popular in recent years is the use of **tillandsias**, usually referred to as 'air plants', as a kind of living sculpture. Tillandsias have clusters of slim, pointed leaves and when mature produce spikes of brightly coloured flowers. They are usually mounted on coral, shells or driftwood, using the same adhesive, and survive by absorbing moisture out of the atmosphere, supplemented usually by a daily misting. Among the bromeliads grown for their interesting leaves are *Aechmea* (which will also flower – see page 81), *Vriesia splendens* (this also produces a flower spike), *neoregelia*, which has cream and green striped leaves or red tinted ones depending on variety, *nidularium*, whose central rosette turns bright red when the plant flowers, and *cryptanthus*, usually called the earth star, the formation of which somewhat resembles a multi-pointed starfish.

Those with attractive flowers include *Billbergia nutans* (see page 81), *vriesia*, *guzmania* and some of the tillandsias. Once most bromeliads have flowered, the central rosette dies off, and a cluster of new rosettes develop around it. These can be detached and potted up separately when, in time, they will make roots into the compost, or left on the plant. It is not really necessary to repot bromeliads until they become top-heavy.

Whereas the **dracaenas** with variegated leaves require good light for the best coloration, some of the green forms will tolerate shade, providing it is not too dense. The ones to look out for are the Madagascar dragon tree, *Dracaena marginata* (narrow leaves with red edges), *D. draco* (the dragon tree) and two closely related **cordylines**, *Cordyline stricta* and *C. australis*, which will even grow outdoors in the summer in warmer parts of Britain. These plants will develop a trunk as they get older. It is quite natural for the bottom leaves to die off eventually, but if the humidity of the room is too low, younger leaves can develop brown tips and yellowing edges. Underwatering can cause brown spotting on the leaves.

Fatsia japonica, which revels under a variety of other names like *Aralia sieboldii*, the Japanese aralia, and the castor oil plant, makes a good specimen subject. It is another which will tolerate almost any situation, but is not keen on too high a temperature as it is really a hardy outdoor plant in most parts of the United Kingdom. It has large, pinnate leaves which can reach more than 12 inches (30 cm) across. There is a good variegated form.

Fatshedera lizei, affectionately referred to sometimes as fat-headed Lizzie, is a hybrid between hedera (ivy) and fatsia, with inherited characteristics from both. Again, it prefers a cool position, and makes a good climbing plant, trained up a moss pole, for the hall or other unheated room, though it can be made into a bushy shrub by pinching out the growing tips.

Ferns are a popular choice for shade, but this conception of their preferences is somewhat inaccurate as many originated on the edge of tropical woodland and, therefore, would receive some dappled sunlight. However, the majority available for home decoration will survive in a range of situations from a north-facing windowsill to the lightly shaded area we are considering here. The preferred temperature is somewhere between 50 and 70°F (13–21°C) – higher than this and the fronds will brown and start to fall off. The compost should be kept moist but not waterlogged, and during summer a very dilute feed must be given at regular intervals. The brown markings which mature ferns develop on the underside of the fronds are not a pest or disease but the spores by which ferns reproduce themselves.

Like so many large groups of plants, there is such a variety of species available for home cultivation at the moment that it would be impossible to go into details about every one, so I shall just list here the general species with some major characteristics. *Adiantum* spp. are the maidenhair ferns, dainty and delicate-looking and not the easiest to grow as they need warmth and high humidity as well as shade. *Asplenium nidus*, the bird's nest fern, has thick, undivided leaves and a fibrous 'nest' in the middle. It must have moist air and the fronds brown off if they are handled. *A. bulbiferum*, the mother fern, looks more like a traditional fern and when mature produces baby plantlets at the edges of its fronds. Nephrolopsis is a big group containing some of our best-known ferns, such as the Boston fern, sword fern, feather fern and lace fern, all with similar herringbone fronds. The button fern, *Pellaea rotundifolia*, has rounded fronds and prefers dry air. *Pellaea viridis*, the green brake fern, is more conventional in appearance and does well in the modern home environment. The staghorn fern, *Platycerium bifurcatum*, has fronds resembling stag's antlers and makes an interesting hanging plant. Pteris includes several increasingly popular small species, often with variegated or intricate fronds, such as the table fern, *Pteris cretica*, its cream variegated cultivar *P. cretica* 'Albolineata', and the cristate table fern *P. cretica* 'Alexandrae'. *P. tremula*, the Australian brake fern, is larger, with long, dainty fronds. The well-known ladder fern, *P. vittata*, is also larger; the leaflets resemble the rungs of a ladder.

The creeping fig, **Ficus pumila**, will take light shade in its stride. It makes good ground cover in a large arrangement and is a good terrarium subject. The stems will cling to most damp surfaces so it will climb slowly, or it can be trained up a moss pole. There is a dwarf form, *Ficus pumila* 'Minima', which has a pleasing variegated version.

Like ferns, **palms** are another huge group which are too numerous to describe in detail here, but which are good specimen plants for light shade. Many will tolerate cool sunshine or brighter conditions, and a few will put up with a little more shade than we are considering, so they are in general very accommodating houseplants. Palms have several distinctive habits. The most popular for home decoration are those with feathery leaves on stems emerging from the centre of the plant, like the Kentia palm (*Howea fosteriana*), sentry palm (*H. belmoreana*), dwarf coconut palm (*Syagrus* or *Cocos weddeliana*), date palms (*Phoenix* spp.), and perhaps the most widely grown of all, the parlour palm (*Chamaedorea elegans*). Another group produces its leaves on top of long canes.

Among those which are commonly available from garden centres are the areca palm (*Chrysalidocarpus lutescens*), the reed palm (*Chamaedorea seifrizii*), and the bamboo palm (*Chamaedorea erumpens*). The other major group has leaves with the individual leaflets spread out like a fan. Many of these are tricky to grow well in the home, but one, *Trachycarpus fortunei*, the windmill palm, is quite obliging and does not get too large. *Chaemaerops humilis*, the European fan palm, is almost hardy and was once seen a lot in the cool conditions of the Victorian drawing room – it needs space so is unsuitable for the smaller room. The sago palm, *Cycas revoluta*, on the other hand, is small and compact and seldom reaches more than 2 feet (0.6 m) in height.

Palms are not difficult to grow, and will often recover when things start to go wrong if steps are taken to correct the problem. Older leaves will naturally turn brown and die; these can be trimmed off. Browning of younger leaves denotes the compost is rather too damp. Too-dry air will cause brown leaf tips; this can be corrected by raising the humidity (page 32). Yellowing leaves are a sign of underwatering.

Marantas are plants with such flamboyant leaves that they make one instinctively feel they must be difficult to grow, whereas all they require is enough water, a reasonably warm position with some moisture in the air, and repotting when they have filled the pot – if this is not done plants start to deteriorate in spite of regular feeding and watering. The three marantas most often seen are *Maranta leuconeura kerchoveana*, the prayer plant or rabbit's foot, which has dark markings on the leaves, *M. leuconeura massangeana* (leaves greenish black with silver main veins and centre), and *M. tricolor*, the herringbone plant, which has similar markings except in red. Marantas have a curious habit: their leaves curl up at night and fold into the centre of the plant. **Stromantha amabilis** is similar to maranta. It is, however, more fussy about warmth and humidity and is happier in a terrarium (see page 114).

Closely related are the **calatheas**, which also have spectacular markings, but the leaves are larger and on thin stalks. *Calathea makoyana*, the peacock plant or cathedral windows (from its semi-transparent appearance), has silver- and green-patterned leaves with red undersides. *C. insignis* (rattlesnake plant) has markings similar to the rabbit's food maranta. Two other kinds you may find are the zebra plant, *C. zebrina*, which has dark stripes running outwards from the midrib, and *C. ornata* (pink, thin stripes). Calatheas are not as easy to grow as maranta because of their papery-thin leaves, and must have plenty of humidity. *Ctenanthe oppenheimiana* 'Tricolor' is very similar – it must be watered with tepid soft water to do well.

Radermachera 'Danielle' is a houseplant you would not have seen in British homes until this decade. It came from Taiwan to Europe about ten years ago, and was first seen on the Continent. It is not the most exciting of plants, being a rather sombre green, but the leaves have a certain attraction as they are compound and have points on the end of each leaflet. It will thrive in light shade or even a bright spot without any sun, but if the light is too low, or if the compost dries out, it will shed its leaflets. You will often find it as a small, bushy plant in garden centres, but a well-grown plant will become quite tall, and so you may have to find a different place for it as it matures.

The mother-in-law's tongue, **sansevieria**, has already been described on page 46 and, although it prefers good natural light, it will put up with some shade. If conditions are too dark the leaves tend to become limp, but the plant will recover if moved to a brighter position.

Tolmiea menziesii, the piggyback plant, will tolerate some shade but is often grown as a hardy herbaceous plant outdoors so it is obvious that it will not be happy with too high temperatures. The common

Detail of Radermachera 'Danielle'

name comes from the plant's habit of sending out trailing stems from the leaves which bear baby plantlets at the ends. It is a small plant with green, downy leaves and a mounded habit. There is a variegated form, but this prefers some sunlight. *T. menziesii* is prone to red spider mite in warm rooms and should therefore be misted regularly.

Moderate shade

This occurs in those parts of a room which are several feet away from the main source of light. You should still be able to read and do some close work here. Exactly where this shade is found depends on the room itself – in one with a large south-facing window it could be as far away as the opposite wall, but in a room with small, sunny windows or a north-facing light it is more likely to be in the vicinity of the centre of the room. The number of plants is much more limited if you want them to thrive on a permanent basis, but many of those in the previous section may live for quite a long time before they begin to look past their best. The plants I am going to suggest here should cause no trouble at all if the other conditions are right for them.

Aglaonema modestum, sometimes called the Chinese evergreen, is an unremarkable-looking green plant not dissimilar in appearance to the aspidistra, which can also be used in places without particularly good natural light. It has long, spear-shaped leaves and occasional, arum-like flowers. It is shallow-rooted, so prefers a shallow container or half-pot. It loves a warm, moist situation so is useful for a shady, well-heated, steamy bathroom. It is prone to red spider mite and mealy bug (see pages 35 and 36). There are some rather more attractive variegated forms such as *A. pseudobracteum*, *A. crispum* and *A. pictum*, which are tolerant of light shade but lose their variegation if placed in too dark a position.

For a cool, shady room, you probably cannot do better than the castor oil plant, **Fatsia japonica**, or the closely related **Fatshedera lizei** (see pages 69 and 70). As one of the parents of fatshedera is *Hedera helix*, English ivy, you can assume that this will stand all but the

Aglaonema modestum

gloomiest spots. Variegated ivies will tend to turn completely green where light levels are low, but if you want something a bit different, you should look for the plain green type of the Canary Island ivy, *Hedera canariensis*, which has a much bigger and smoother leaf. This is usually found in its variegated form 'Gloire de Marengo', but sometimes the green variety can be picked up from the outdoor climbing plant section of garden centres. If the room is fairly warm and it has been growing outside, you should get it used to indoor conditions gradually as it may otherwise drop its leaves and turn brown.

Another climbing plant I find grows quite well in light shade is *Philodendron scandens*, the sweetheart plant. Some of the other philodendrons (see pages 63–64) and even monstera are worth a try, but may need more light in winter, so if the plant is very large it is a good idea to stand it on a base with casters. This advice also applies to large containers permanently planted with arrangements of houseplants. They can be extremely heavy, and there will be times when you may want to move them, when cleaning the room, for instance, or if they appear to need more or less light.

Fittonia is one of the only variegated – or what appears to be variegated – plants which thrive in shade. The most commonly grown is *Fittonia argyroneura* 'Nana', the snakeskin plant, which appears at first glance to be variegated green and white but is, in fact, a green-leaved plant with all the veins picked out in white, giving it the appearance of being covered in net. There is a bigger form, *F. argyroneura*, the silver net or nerve plant, and a less well-known species, *F. verschaffeltii*, which is similar, but the veins are red. The snakeskin plant is the easiest to grow as a houseplant as it will tolerate less humidity than the other two, which require constant warmth, high humidity, moist compost and no draughts, so are more suited to the terrarium (see page 114). The snakeskin plant has a creeping habit, so young plants can be produced by providing pots of compost for the stems to root into. Once a good root system has formed, the new plants can be severed from their parents.

This type of shade is about as far as we can go with plants for sunless conditions, as there are virtually none which will tolerate deep shade. For a temporary effect, you could try some of the suggestions from these last two sections, though these should remain for a short period only and be removed to a more favourable place before they show signs of deterioration. Plants taken out of their regular environment in this way should not be moved around too often; they must be given plenty of time to settle down again. It is as well to have a good supply to draw from.

Rooms with no regular form of heat

In the modern homes of today in the United Kingdom and other parts of northern Europe, the unheated room in winter is somewhat of a thing of the past – speaking generally, at any rate. However, in larger houses, where it is uneconomical to heat every room all the time, one can still find areas where it is predominantly very cool, the temperature only rising perhaps a few times during the winter period. This is not necessarily detrimental to many plants, the only ones likely to take offence being those from tropical regions of the world where warmth and humidity are essential to survival. The main things to remember are that plants from sub-tropical regions are not likely to thrive at temperatures below 45°F (7°C), watering will need to be watched carefully, the plants will be in a state of full dormancy during the shortest months of the year and so will not require any feeding, and that, just as in other parts of the home with higher temperatures plants have individual preferences regarding light and shade, so do they still in cooler conditions.

There are many species cultivated as houseplants which are almost hardy in temperate regions, and will survive, sometimes to advantage, much colder situations providing the temperature does not drop below freezing point. Among these are many indoor flowering plants, which will last much longer in this environment. One obvious example of these are spring bulbs grown in pots and bowls for indoor decoration (see page 66), which are usually hardy outside anyway, but there are many other instances just as successful.

A few conifers can look quite decorative in this kind of area where the light is bright enough to prevent them looking washed out. Many garden species can be used, but there is one species, **Araucaria heterophylla**, the Norfolk Island pine, which is actually sold as a houseplant in this country as it is not hardy out of doors. A relative of the widely planted monkey puzzle tree, it is slow growing, with stiff branches covered with rigid needles radiating symmetrically from a central trunk. Although it will survive warmer temperatures, it needs misting if the air is dry, and therefore is eminently suitable for a light, cool area where it makes an excellent, undemanding specimen.

The **aspidistra**, of course, had to tolerate this kind of situation for a century of cultivation in the home, and tolerated it very well indeed. In a cold room it will require virtually no watering in winter. Cultural hints are on page 68. The unheated room is really too chilly for the variegated form.

The indoor azalea, **Azalea simsii**, which used to be known as *Azalea indica*, has been known to survive the winter outside in warmer parts of Britain, but the poor thing is so often expected to survive hot, stuffy living rooms; all too often it does not, and the leaves fall and the buds brown and fail to open, especially when the transition from the cool moist nursery greenhouse to the home environment is made too rapidly. What it really likes is a frost-free, light position and a lime-free compost which is never allowed to dry out. Watering should be with soft water, though if this is impossible, you can usually get away with tap water if a houseplant feed with chelated trace elements is used (see page 24). After flowering, and when the outside air temperature has warmed up somewhat, the indoor azalea can be put outside (in its pot) in a semi-shaded spot for the summer. Again, it should always be kept well watered, especially when the buds are forming in late summer.

Azaleas are repotted only when root-bound if you want a continuity of flower production, as the year after repotting they often make growth rather than flowers. I am often asked if it is possible to prune an indoor azalea. The answer is that you will not kill it, but pruning back should only be done if the plant has become very bare and straggly, as you will trim off the wherewithal for the plant to make next year's flowers, which are initiated just under the old flower head of the current season. Because of this, dead-heading should also be done with care, removing just the spent flower head and no more. It should be remembered that an indoor azalea is a small, woody shrub, and it is natural for it to develop a woody, leafless base in time. Given the right growing conditions, this does not detract in any way from the performance of the plant.

It is not generally appreciated just how low the temperature can fall for **cacti** and **succulents** (see pages 41 and 42) still to survive, and yet providing they are not allowed to freeze (as the large amounts of water will expand and burst the tissue) they can stand rooms which are much too cold to sit or work in, provided they have as much light as you can give them throughout the winter. In fact, given this large differential between winter and summer temperatures, and a full resting period, they are much more likely to produce flowers on a regular basis.

Calceolaria herbeohybrida, the slipper flower, with its balloon-shaped flowers of red, orange, yellow or white blotched with a dark colour, was a very popular temporary flowering houseplant a few years ago, but seems to have slipped from the ratings somewhat recently. This is possibly due to the fact that it is in flower during the spring, usually before we have plucked up courage to reduce or turn off the central heating, and so many living rooms are too warm for the plant to give value for money – like the **cineraria** (see page 59) it soon shows signs of stress and the flowers fade quickly if it is too hot. In an unheated room, especially if the plant is bought while it still has plenty of buds on it, you can expect it to last happily for several weeks. The indoor **pot chrysanthemum** (see page 50) will also appreciate the lower temperatures, but all three of these must be given the best light possible during the early months of the year or moulds may rot the flowers.

There are few people who do not instantly recognize the spider plant, *Chlorophytum comosum* '**Vittatum**' and *C.c.* 'Variegatum', with its grass-like, cream and green, longitudinally striped leaves and arching stems either bearing white flowers or baby plantlets. In my own home I have had spider plants in every position from above a central heating radiator to the windowsill of an unheated outside WC without having too many problems in any place. It is, in fact, happiest in a very cool spot in an east or west light in summer, and in any sunny, frost-free place in winter; if the air is too hot and dry some browning of the ends of the leaves will occur but this can be trimmed off to make the plant look better. In poor light, the leaves will gradually turn pale and flaccid.

You won't kill a chlorophytum with an occasional overwatering, but you can if it is left constantly standing in water, as the fleshy, tuber-like roots will start to rot, though if the damage is not too bad the affected parts can be trimmed off and the plant will generally recover. Propagation is by rooting the plantlets in small pots of compost while still on the parent and detaching them when they are growing on their own root system. Large plants can be split carefully in spring, but the resultant new ones may be lop-sided for some time.

The indoor cyclamen, *Cyclamen persicum*, is an ideal plant for a cool position in a good light but away from very strong sunshine.

It will flower for months on end, but it will, of course, require much less water than in a warm room. Cultural details are found on page 59.

I have mentioned several times already (see pages 69, 70, 74) how adaptable are **fatshedera** and its parents **fatsia** and **hedera**, the ivy. *Fatsia japonica*, the castor oil plant, will tolerate some shade and even a degree or two of frost; its variegated forms 'Variegata' and 'Albo-marginata', which is very similar, need a better light to keep their coloration. *Fatshedera lizei* seems to prefer a slightly warmer environment – not below 40°F (4.5°C) – and the variegated cultivar is not really suitable for rooms which are totally unheated at all times. Ivies, being in the main hardy plants, will be delighted not to be over-cooked, but again, the more pronounced the variegation, the more the light that will be necessary to maintain it.

Grevillea robusta, the silk oak, grows as a large, evergreen tree in the warmer parts of the United States, but was once very popular as a houseplant in Europe. It seemed to disappear from view a few years ago, but now more garden centres appear to be stocking it again. It is tolerant of most temperatures and situations, will stand some direct sunlight, but will also grow in light shade, and is perhaps best grown in an unheated, light position as it will not out-grow its place so rapidly. The plant sheds its ferny leaves as it matures, but can be kept more juvenile by cutting back when it has grown 2–3 feet (0.6–0.9 m). It is easily raised from seed, so it is a good idea to throw away older plants and replace with young ones.

It is surprising how the variously coloured hybrids of **primrose** and **polyanthus** have become popular as houseplants, as to my mind they are quite unsuitable for the majority of homes. They are quite hardy, liking the cool conditions of the temperate spring, and prefer a partially shaded, moist spot to one in full sunlight with dry ground. And yet they are expected to flourish when brought in from the cool or cold greenhouse to the stuffy, centrally heated living room – the flowers soon fade and the plants need an immediate breath of fresh air if they are to be saved for another season. However, in a light, unheated environment indoors they make quite satisfactory flowering pot plants, as does an old-fashioned 'cottage garden' relative, *Primula* 'Gold Lace', which will flower for weeks on end in a cool, light position. The flowers are unmistakable, yellow-centred, with an almost black, single ring of petals fringed with gold, and the plant can be grown permanently in the garden after its use as indoor decoration, as can the other primroses and polyanthuses.

On the other hand, some types of primula are slightly tender, and have been grown successfully for many years as flowering pot plants. The most common are the fairy primrose, *Primula malacoides*, *P. obconica*, the Chinese primrose, *P. sinensis*, and *P. kewensis*. *P. malacoides* is scented, with dainty pink, purple, or red flowers arranged in whorls up the stems rather like those of the outdoor candelabra primula. *P. obconica* should not be grown by people who are prone to allergies and rashes, as it can produce a nasty skin eruption in some persons. It is, nevertheless, very attractive, with larger heads of fragrant flowers in many colours. *P. sinensis* is not as universally grown – it has primrose-like flowers with frilly petals, and large leaves with toothed edges. *P. kewensis* is yellow-flowered and looks somewhat like an oxlip.

As temporary decoration they are usually thrown away after flowering, but can be saved from year to year if repotted immediately after flowering and grown on in a cool, light position through the summer. Many of the leaves will become rather tatty, just as they do in their garden counterparts, but can be tidied up in the autumn before the flower buds start to form. The best plants are those raised annually from seed sown in June.

Saxifraga sarmentosa is a plant which most people would recognize but few would be able to name, and is sometimes called (ambiguously, as are so many other houseplants) mother-of-thousands. The plant is insignificant, typically saxifrage-like, but it has the distinction of producing many thin red runners with baby plants on the ends, which will grow into new ones if potted up individually. Its preferred spot is a light one which is on the cool side, and it will survive the winter with no heat at all if the watering is watched. Accommodatingly, it will also tolerate warmer places and therefore makes a good hanging specimen. There is a much more attractive variegated form ('Tricolor') which is variegated cream with red edges, but this requires some heat in winter to keep it at its best.

I have already recommended tolmiea on page 72 as being a good plant for a lightly shaded area; being fairly hardy it will also thrive where there is no heat in the room. The variegated form will need a lighter position than the all-green one.

The centrally heated room

As we have already seen on pages 31–33, central heating can be one of the real enemies of houseplants, drying the air excessively to cause moisture loss on a large scale, and also tending to keep them in weak, spindly growth during the shortest months of the year when what they should be having is a well-earned rest. At best, plants objecting to central heating will develop browning and drying out of leaf edges and margins, yellowing and leaf loss; at worst, eventually they will die unless steps are taken to improve the environment – such as misting of both the upper surface and underside of the leaves, grouping, and creating a damp microclimate with an outer container of moist material or by standing the pots on a tray of damp gravel. There is, however, a limited selection of houseplants which, although not at their happiest in conditions of hot, dry air, will put up with it without undue detriment.

Cacti and **succulents** are obviously one group, as they carry their own supply of water. Some **bromeliads** will also survive in dry air – not all, as many of them originated in areas of high humidity.

Bromeliads will tolerate centrally heated conditions if they are regularly misted, and although some drying of the leaf ends may occur, the effect of central heating is not usually fatal. There are two particular plants in this group which are impervious to central heating: aechmea and *Billbergia nutans*.

Aechmea fasciata is the true urn plant, though some people refer to all bromeliads with a water-collecting receptacle in the centre as urn plants. It is an eye-catching plant with long, thick, strap-like leaves with serrated edges of a silvery-green colour. A flower head comprising rose-red bracts and small, blue, true flowers is produced from the centre of the mature rosette, which afterwards usually dies, to be replaced by a ring of smaller rosettes. Another two aechmeas some-times to be found in garden centres are – *A. chantinii*, the Amazonian zebra plant, which has a flower spike composed of orange bracts and yellow flowers, and *A. fulgens* 'Discolor', otherwise known as the coral berry, which has purple undersides to the leaves, purple flowers and red berries. Aechmeas are watered by filling the 'urn' in the middle with soft, tepid water – this built-in water carrier should not dry out.

Billbergia nutans (common names are queen's tears or friend-ship plant) has reddish-tinted grassy leaves and drooping flower heads.

Curiously enough, although central heating will not affect bilbergia, it will withstand very low temperatures, so can be used where a very low overall temperature is maintained – as long as the light is good.

The other plants which can be used without effort in centrally heated rooms we have already looked at elsewhere in this book. I mentioned on page 78 that I grew a **Chlorophytum comosum** (spider plant) for many years adjacent to a very hot radiator. Apart from watering daily and periodically trimming off the dead leaf ends it needed no other attention.

Most of the green-leaved **dracaenas** (see page 69) will also perform reasonably well, though those with variegated leaves are inclined to turn brown where the variegations are most pronounced. The red-leaved relative, *Cordyline terminalis*, is not quite so adaptable, and can develop brown patches if the air is very dry, but it responds well to misting.

Two members of the fig family, **Ficus benjamina**, the weeping fig, and **F. pumila**, the creeping fig (see pages 60 and 71), are also suitable for centrally heated rooms. You can tell if you have over-stepped the mark with excessive heat or air dryness as they will shed their younger leaves; a daily spraying with tepid water should correct this.

That obliging duo, **monstera** and **philodendron** (see pages 61 and 63), have cropped up in just about every section of this book, being able to take a wide range of conditions in their stride. Here they are again, because, in addition to all their other attributes, they will also tolerate central heating. **Radermachera 'Danielle'** (see page 72) looks as though it will be joining them in future lists of accommodating plants, as the dark green, leathery leaves of this species also seem to cope with air containing too little moisture for the well-being of the majority of plants.

Peperomias are worth a try in a centrally heated atmosphere. Their leaves cope well with dry air, even though their original home was the floor of the South American jungle. Their fleshy leaves apparently are able to contain and hang onto enough water to keep them from being stressed. (See pages 62 to 63 for recommended varieties and cultural details.)

Another succulent type which I have already recommended as being suitable for a position in full sun (see page 45), is the ivy-leaved form of **senecio**, *S. macroglossus*, the Cape ivy, and its closely related species *S. mikanioides*, the German ivy, which makes an ideal trailing or climbing

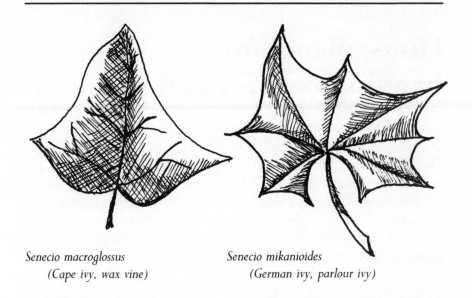

Senecio macroglossus
(Cape ivy, wax vine)

Senecio mikanioides
(German ivy, parlour ivy)

Leaf Forms

plant in dry air, where the true ivies would start shedding their leaves. (Further details are to be found on page 88.)

Remember that, although when we talk about centrally heated rooms we generally think about water-filled radiators heated by a boiler, you can get the same dry air conditions where night storage heaters, convector stoves and oil-filled or panel radiators are installed. Especially dry air can be produced where electric fan heaters are regularly used.

Houseplants for
hanging baskets and pots

There are many species of plants suitable for indoor cultivation and with an attractively lax habit, which make eminently suitable specimens in hanging baskets and pots. The choice of containers these days is enormous, ranging from the simplest adaptation of the ordinary plant pot converted into a hanging pot with a clip-on plastic hanger and drip tray, through a wide range of ceramic, terracotta, brass, copper and wickerwork hanging containers, to the plastic outdoor hanging basket capable of holding several plants in an arrangement. Hanging plants can also be displayed effectively from wrought iron wall-mounted holders, though the results will, of course, be one-sided.

Introducing houseplants into a room in this way creates a pleasing, restful effect, but there are certain points to remember. The most tempting way of fixing them up is, as I mentioned in the Introduction, by putting a hook in the ceiling, but this can be fraught with danger unless you know exactly where your joists are, so it is usually wiser to adopt some other method. If it is not going to get in the way of any curtain fittings, one method is to put up a wooden curtain pole somewhere near the window – this is usually only feasible where there are no curtains or they are hung inside the reveal. It has the advantage of being able to hold several plants, but if there is a long run of pole it will need intermediate brackets to prevent it sagging. It is more often practical to suspend the pot from an ornamental wall bracket specially designed for the purpose; there are many good designs around, but they must be strong enough to cope with the weight of the plant when well-grown and newly watered. If plants are to trail from a shelf, the pot should be heavy enough or anchored firmly.

Like other houseplants, you should always make sure that your chosen site and the plant are compatible; it is possibly even more tempting to fit a certain subject in with the decor when it is such a noticeable feature in a room. Hanging pots should always be positioned where they do not get in the way – remember, it may be above *your* head, but are there likely to be taller people using the room? The plant will generally need to be low enough to be watered with ease – unless you invest in a hanging basket pulley – so it will have to be reasonably out of the way or you will be constantly walking into it. It is also wise not to have anything too special underneath, particularly if there is only a shallow drip-tray attached to the pot. If the inner pot is placed in an outer container of the same depth (which is better as far as the risk of water running over is concerned), it should be checked regularly to ensure surplus water is not being allowed to remain there.

A very effective arrangement, where a suitable fixing point can be provided, is to use a macramé hanger capable of holding several plants in tiers. This can be positioned towards a light corner of the room and if the right plants are chosen it can look quite spectacular, especially if some trailing species are trained to grow upwards on the macramé. Thought has to be given as to the plants to use; the stronger-growing ones with a more dense habit should be nearer to the bottom so they do not smother more moderate varieties.

The following list is by no means exhaustive, but gives a good selection for most situations in the home.

The lipstick vine, **aeschynanthus**, is a plant which is often recognized but seldom named. There are two species which go under the common name, *Aeschynanthus lobbianus* and *A. speciosus*, though strictly speaking it is the former which is the true lipstick vine, this name being derived from the shape of the red flowers with a brown calyx. *A. speciosus* makes a larger plant, with striking red and yellow flowers. It is often confused with **columnea**, the goldfish plant, which it resembles both in foliage and flowers. *Columnea gloriosa* and *C. banksii* are the two most commonly found for sale; they, like aeschynanthus, must have a humid position in bright light to succeed, so are often candidates for hanging over the kitchen sink or cooker, where they usually seem to do very well; a light, well-used bathroom is also suitable.

If you are looking for something less exacting in requirements, **Asparagus densiflorus sprengeri** (see page 58) might be more in your line. This will tolerate a much wider range of light levels and temperatures. I had one growing for many years on a pedestal above a very deep, though light, stairwell, where it eventually touched the floor, having made about ten feet of trailing growth. When the plant gets as large as this, it tends to shed its needle-like foliage constantly, so it can be a nuisance.

Campanula isophylla is a slightly tender relation to the low-growing alpine bell-flowers and makes a good perennial flowering plant for a hanging pot. It has large blue or white flowers and propagates easily from division in spring. A light, not-too-warm spot is ideal; it also makes a good constituent of an outdoor hanging basket in summer.

Ceropegia woodii, the rosary vine or string of hearts, is a popular, dainty hanging plant with trailing, wiry stems which can be 3 feet (0.9 m) or more long, and heart-shaped green and silver leaves with purple undersides. It is not immediately recognizable as a succulent plant, until you look at the small leaves closely; they are fleshy and therefore the plant is suitable for areas where the air tends to be warm and dry.

The spider plant, **Chlorophytum comosum 'Vittatum'** (see page 78), should not be condemned as a hanging basket plant because it is so widely grown – a mature specimen can reach several feet across and looks magnificent where space allows. In a very warm room, the brown leaf-ends should be trimmed off regularly to improve the appearance.

There are two species of **fern** which will grow in a hanging container to effect, though the air should not be too hot and dry. The first is **Nephrolepis exaltata**, which is best known for the variety 'Bostoniensis', the Boston fern, but there are several others whose fronds will hang over the side of the pot in time. The other is **Platycerium bifurcatum**, the staghorn fern (see page 70). This is not so much a hanging plant as one which should be hung up, as in its native Australia it grows on tree trunks. It can therefore be attached to a piece of log by removing it from its pot and tying on the moss-covered rootball with thin training wire. The log is then suspended from the ceiling by chains. It is watered by immersing it about once a week. After a few minutes it is removed, hung up somewhere to drain, and then repositioned in its permanent spot. You will sometimes hear the maidenhair fern, **Adiantum caudatum**, recommended as a hanging plant. Although the habit is suitable, it is not an easy plant to grow out of the terrarium and seldom succeeds in the home as a hanging houseplant.

Three members of the fig family, **Ficus**, make excellent specimens in hanging pots. They are *Ficus pumila* (the creeping fig) and its smaller counterpart, *F. pumila* 'Minima' (including the variegated form – see

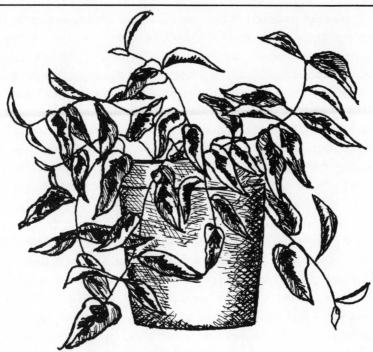

Ficus radicans 'Variegata' (trailing fig)

page 71) and the trailing fig, *F. radicans*, which is more popular in its trailing form 'Variegata'. This has larger leaves than *F. pumila*, wiry, trailing stems, and the variegated form is heavily margined in creamy-yellow. With all these trailing forms, severe damage can occur if they are exposed to bright sunshine.

One plant which seems to have become very popular as a trailing houseplant in the last few years is the variegated ground ivy, **Glechoma hederacea 'Variegata'**, which is surprising in a way, as it is hardy outdoors in most parts of the United Kingdom. It is the plant which is usually sold by garden centres as trailing nepeta, and is used extensively in summer hanging baskets. It has long, trailing stems and slightly hairy leaves variegated with white, which are aromatic. It prefers a cool, light spot indoors and can become rather straggly in time, so periodic trimming back is necessary.

Another easy plant, which can either be used as a climber or a trailer, depending on how it is trained, is **Gynura sarmentosa**, sometimes called the velvet plant. It will even grow in direct sunlight, so is a useful hanging plant for a bright window area or sunny porch. It has nettle-shaped leaves covered with purple hairs, and small yellow flowers which are best removed as they have a rather unpleasant smell. Older plants become straggly, but the shape can be improved by pinching out the growing tips at regular intervals. Cuttings taken in spring and summer root very easily and it is a good idea to keep a supply of young plants coming on with which to replace the rather untidy older ones.

I have mentioned **ivies** in other parts of this book; their versatility extends in situations of low humidity, to their making first-rate basket subjects, but the air must be cool and buoyant, otherwise leaf-browning and leaf-drop will occur. A good effect can be achieved by planting several varieties with different leaf colours and forms in the same basket, *Senecio macroglossus* and *S. mikanioides*.

Helxine soleirolii, or mind-your-own-business, is more often seen as a ground cover plant under the bench of old-established green-houses – it will also grow outside. However, in a cool room it makes a good plant for a hanging pot providing it is misted to keep the atmosphere around it moist. Care should be taken that bits of it do not become detached and re-rooted into an indoor garden type of plant combination, as it can become a nuisance, growing and spreading rapidly to become a pernicious weed. There is a gold-leaved form, and also a pretty silvery cultivar, 'Argentea'. The compost must not be allowed to dry out or browning will occur.

Most **kalanchoës** are upright-growing succulent plants but a pendulous form has recently come onto the gardening scene. *Kalanchoë* 'Tessa' has small, shiny leaves resembling in shape the flaming Katy (see page 43), and pendant, tubular flowers of an unusual peach colour. It is an excellent early summer flowering plant, but again, with light control in the nursery, plants in flower can be obtained at other times of the year. The cultivation is the same as for other forms of kalanchoë grown for their flowering effect (see page 43).

The **marantas** (see page 71), are usually trained upright when the stems begin to trail, but they can equally effectively be displayed in a hanging pot. Where the air is warm and dry, daily misting will be necessary.

Pelargonium peltatum, the ivy-leaved, trailing form of bedding geranium (see page 44) is usually grown out of doors in summer, but there is no reason why it should not be used as an indoor hanging plant. There are many varieties available, some with the added bonus of variegated leaves. Plenty of sun is essential, and the plants should flower nearly all the time if the position is bright enough. It is a good hanging subject for areas where many other plants would find it too sunny, hot and dry.

There are a few trailing forms of **peperomia** which are suitable for basket planting in centrally heated locations in semi-shade. *Peperomia scandens* 'Variegata' can sometimes be mistaken for the trailing fig, but the leaf edges are smooth, not wavy, and the stalks are pink. The variegation is also a deeper gold. *P. rotundifolia* has round, succulent green leaves. The creeping peperomia, *P. prostrata*, is sometimes confused with *Ceropegia woodii* as the green leaves marked with silver are very similar, but the stems of *P. prostrata* are less straggly.

The aluminium plant family, **pilea** (see page 64), has a few notable trailing species. *Pilea nummulariifolia*, or creeping Charlie, is a small plant with deeply indented veins and red stems. *P. depressa*, creeping Jenny, is another small-leaved form, whereas *P. spruceana* 'Norfolk', while creeping attractively down the sides of the container, is very different, with leaves much more like the aluminium plant, but with bronze markings. Good light is essential, but these plants should be kept out of strong summer sunshine.

Plectranthus, the Swedish ivy, is another plant which is accommodating enough to grow outside quite successfully in summer, and the variegated form, *Plectranthus coleoides* 'Marginatus', which has a white edging to the leaves, is becoming increasingly popular as a foliage subject in outdoor summer hanging baskets. Most of the commonly available forms seem to be referred to as Swedish ivy, whereas there are several distinctly different species around. *P. coleoides* 'Marginatus' has a hairy leaf surface. *P. oertendahlii* has leaf veins picked out in white, and a purple underside. *P. australis*, the plant usually passed from person to person as cuttings and frequently found for sale at coffee mornings and sales of work, has a dark green leaf with a waxy coating. Swedish ivy is easy to grow – the plain green forms do not care for direct sunshine but the variegated one will stand quite a lot, especially if grown outdoors or in an airy place inside.

Saxifraga sarmentosa and its variegated form have already been described in some detail on page 80. They are perhaps best seen as free-hanging specimens when, even suspended quite high up, the all-green type will sometimes reach the floor, although the pink-edged cream and green variety is more moderate of habit.

I once acquired that most peculiar plant **Senecio rowleyanus**, the string of beads plant, by mistake. I was bidding in an auction at the end of a local horticultural society's annual show for what I thought was a particularly nice pelargonium, but through some mistake I actually ended up with the string of beads. This is another plant which illustrates the enormous versatility of this large genus of plants. It comprises long, lax, thread-like stems to which are attached along the length round, bead-like, succulent leaves. These stems are capable of becoming several feet long in time, but can be trimmed back. The trimmings can be separated into short pieces and inserted into potting compost which has been opened up with the addition of some sharp sand, and they will root readily. Unfortunately, it is very prone to infestation with whitefly, but regular spraying with a houseplant insecticide should deal with this. There are two other similar forms of senecio – S. herreianus, which has oval, bead-like leaves, and S. citriformis, with lemon-shaped foliage.

The piggyback plant, **Tolmiea menziesii**, has been described in detail on page 72. It is a very good hanging plant for an unheated room, porch or conservatory. The golden-leaved form is particularly attractive in a hanging pot in a semi-shaded or reasonably bright place.

The common trailing **tradescantia** was my first introduction to houseplants. Tradescantia albiflora straggled from a pot on my form-mistress's desk and was held up to us as an example of a bomb-proof indoor plant. (It must be to have grown in that position, thinking back on it!) As a species it is pretty boring, but it grows well from cuttings and there are some good variegated forms around like T. albiflora 'Albovittata' with white and green striped leaves, 'Aurea' with golden leaves, and 'Tricolor', where the leaves are striped with white and purple. Similar to T. albiflora 'Albovittata' is T. fluminensis 'Quicksilver', and 'Variegata', which is cream-striped. T. blossfeldiana 'Variegata' has a larger leaf, white stripes and a purple tint and leaf undersurface.

There are several closely related species which for convenience are often known as tradescantia but strictly speaking are not. **Zebrina pendula** is very similar to Tradescantia blossfeldiana 'Variegata', but the leaf surface of zebrina is shiny whereas that of tradescantia is dull. Z. pendula 'Purpusii' is striped green and purple; 'Quadricolor' is variegated green, pink, red and silver. The flowers of zebrina are produced in summer and are small and purple, those of tradescantia are usually insignificant and white.

Callisia elegans, which is also sometimes known as **Setcreasea striata**, has smaller leaves than those of the zebrina and the white stripes are thinner and more regular. The leaf surface is dull, more like that of tradescantia, and the underleaf is reddish-purple. *Callisia fragrans* is similar, but in bright light the leaves turn pink. Sometimes known as the purple tradescantia or purple heart is another related species, **Setcreasea purpurea**, which has hairy purple leaves, pink flowers, and an increasingly untidy habit as the plant grows older. It is better to take cuttings regularly of the young material and discard the parents when they begin to look too straggly.

Tradescantias and their relatives need good light to prevent spindly growth. A good shape can be maintained by pinching back the growth tips regularly, but young plants always look the best. They require plenty of water in summer, otherwise the leaves turn yellow, and low humidity causes them to brown, so they are not good plants for a very dry atmosphere. Sometimes all-green, strong-growing shoots are produced; these should be removed as soon as noticed to prevent them 'taking over' the plant.

Plants for the inveterate overwaterer

The commonest cause of houseplant failure as far as the inexperienced grower is concerned is overwatering. There seems to be this idea that a little drop of water will do them good, and a lot of water will do them more good, but as I have already explained in some detail in the Introduction, nothing could be further from the truth. Waterlogged soil causes root rotting and the inability of the plant to absorb efficiently any nutrients contained in the compost. Plants have their own specific needs – some are capable of dealing with a larger volume of water than others, but as a general rule the compost should be nicely moist, not bone dry or over-wet, and does not need another watering until the surface feels dry to the touch. However, if you know that nothing gives you greater pleasure than to wander around with a watering can in your hand, or you want to buy a houseplant for someone who drowns everything he or she attempts to grow, there are a very few pot plants which will actually put up with waterlogging and standing water, and although the small number of these narrows down the selection a great deal, they are good-looking plants in their own right, and can also make an interesting change for anyone else.

Acorus graminus, which is usually grown as a houseplant in its variegated form 'Variegatus', is a grassy plant which is fairly hardy and grows well as a marginal subject in the boggy area at the side of a sunny pool. It is unhappy in warm rooms and, if the air is too dry, is prone to red spider mite, so should be misted with water as a precaution. The compost is kept wet at all times, and it should be given a position in good light, but away from direct sun if the room is warm. It should be kept in an unheated place in winter.

Azalea simsii is described on page 97; like acorus, it likes nothing better than a light, unheated room and plenty of water, which, if you intend to use the plant for more than just temporary decoration, should be lime-free to prevent lime-induced chlorosis. Where there is some heat in the room, regular misting when the plant is in bud is

Acorus graminus 'Variegatus'
(sweet flag)

helpful, sometimes as much as twice a day. Again, the compost should be wet rather than damp, but the base of the pot should not remain in standing water as, unlike acorus and some other species I am about to mention, the roots are not sufficiently adapted to cope with a very waterlogged situation.

Carex is another grassy plant with much in common with acorus. The variety usually grown as a houseplant is *Carex morrowii* 'Variegata', again a hardy plant, which is also known as the Japanese sedge. I have one growing in a damp but by no means waterlogged part of the garden in dappled sunlight; it will tolerate other light levels from bright sun to light shade, however, provided the compost is kept constantly moist in warm, bright spots. It will even stand an occasional drying out, but the roots cannot cope with being in permanently saturated compost. *C. morrowii* 'Variegata' resembles the spider plant in many respects, but is altogether a more dainty plant and it does not produce runners.

Cyperus, the umbrella plant, *loves* standing water; the outer container should always be kept topped up in addition to the compost being wet. *Cyperus papyrus*, from which paper was obtained in Biblical times, is sometimes grown as a houseplant, and is probably the most attractive of those available for indoor cultivation, with very thin leaves making up a mop-head of foliage on top of stems which can reach 8 feet (2.5 m) and more, so it is not a plant for the small home. It is also not particularly easy to grow as it is rather fussy about over-dry air. The most suitable cyperus for home cultivation is *C. diffusus*, which seldom reaches more than 2 feet (0.6 m) and has a parasol of leaves radiating from the top of the stems and small, grass-like flowers in summer (cyperus is, in fact, another member of the sedge family). *C. alternifolia* looks very much the same, but gets much taller – up to 4 feet (1.2 m). The two best forms to look out for are 'Gracilis', which is smaller and more compact, and 'Variegatus', with dark green leaves striped white.

Cyperus alternifolia 'Gracilis' (dwarf umbrella plant)

Cyperus needs a minimum temperature of around 50°F (10°C), and misting helps to stop the leaf-ends browning in summer. Hot sun can be harmful.

I suppose part of the popularity of **impatiens** (busy lizzie – see page 51) is its love of moisture, as it is easier to kill it with underwatering than by giving it too much. The compost should be very moist in summer, but less water should be given in winter when the plant is not in active growth. The most pleasing plants are the newer F_1 and F_2 hybrids, which are more compact with larger flowers – such as 'Imp' (dwarf), 'Novette' (very dwarf), 'Rosette' (double and semi-double flowers like miniature roses), 'Blitz' (dwarf and particularly free-flowering) and 'Zig-Zag' (candy-striped flowers). These are all easily grown from seed, which is available in single colours of red, orange, pink and white, or in mixtures.

The 'New Guinea Hybrids' were developed from *Impatiens hawkeri* and *I. linearifolia*. They grow much taller, making eye-catching plants, with narrow leaves variegated yellow and green, or bronze, or yellow, red and green, depending on the cultivar, and bright red or pink flowers contrasting well with the foliage.

Very much like the busy lizzie, but with larger flowers which resemble camellias, are the **balsams** (*Impatiens balsamina*). Most grow to around 18 inches (46 cm), but there is a dwarf form called 'Tom Thumb'. Cultivation is similar to that for busy lizzies and these are also easily raised from seed. Another impatiens species sometimes seen in garden centres, and which to my mind has more of a curiosity value than an aesthetic one, is 'Parrot Beak'. It makes a rather stiff plant with odd flowers resembling the beak of a parrot, coloured red and yellow.

Back to the grasses, there is yet another which will tolerate very wet compost, providing it is not waterlogged. This is **Scirpus cernuus**, the miniature bulrush. Closely related to some of our outdoor marginal water plants, this one requires a slightly higher temperature in winter than can be found out-of-doors in Britain, so makes a good indoor plant. It has bright green, glossy, gracefully slender leaves (which are actually hollow stems); these grow upright at first and then start to arch over, making the plant visually suitable for many places, especially in a hanging pot or trailing over the edge of a container of mixed plants. Some nurseries even turn it into a miniature standard by growing the stems through a narrow tube. Bright light, though not direct sun, is essential, and where the air is dry, regular misting should be given.

The heated conservatory

To talk of 'the heated conservatory' is rather akin to discussing the length of a piece of string – what, exactly, are we talking about when we say 'heated'? Just how warm is this vague term?

Going back to when fuel was comparatively cheap and conservatories were usually owned by people who had the money to spend on heat, 'heated' could often refer to 'stove house' conditions, where the temperature would be as warm as our living rooms today, and much more humid. The plants which could be grown under such conditions were almost unlimited, and would include most of those we struggle to keep healthy as warmth-loving houseplants – in older gardening books you will actually see these kinds referred to as 'stove' plants. Indeed, where heating costs are no object today, there is nothing to prevent one from keeping the temperature around 65–70°F (18–21°C) in winter, and more in summer, in which case most of the houseplants we have looked at already would thrive, especially where the humidity could be kept high.

Lowering the temperature 10°F (5°C) would still mean that a wide selection of popular houseplants could be grown, especially if watering were considerably reduced in winter. Certain plants – for example, crotons and calathea – would, however, find life a struggle.

Bearing in mind the high cost of fuel today, and the fact that because the large area of glass, even if double-glazed, means that to keep a conservatory or garden room at the same temperature as a conventional living room with brick or stone walls and only one or two windows requires the consumption of considerably more energy, perhaps the most practical temperature is around 50°F (10°C) in winter and 70°F (21°C) in summer. This will give plenty of scope, but would exclude plants originating from very hot, steamy jungle areas of the world.

Ideally, a conservatory should have plenty of height to allow the cultivation of larger plants, but I realize that some 'sun-rooms' are more like the other rooms of the home but with more glass. This would restrict the choice to the compact, 'houseplant' types, which are

The piggy-back plant *(Tolmeia menziesii)* makes a useful hanging plant for a light, unheated place *(above)*
The Boston fern *(below left)* likes a humid position
A successful basket of ivy in a cool window *(below right)*

The staghorn fern *(above)* can be attached to a piece of wood to form an interesting hanging feature

The lipstick vine *(below)* prefers warmth and humidity

perhaps best displayed on shelving or staging, the larger ones standing on the floor. The Victorian-style conservatory is usually much taller. If conditions allow and you are constructing one from scratch, it is a good idea to have proper beds, which may have to be raised to allow drainage, so the plants can grow directly in these, giving a more natural appearance. Larger conservatories may even be able to accommodate a pool and fountain, which helps the humidity considerably and greatly adds to the effect, especially if you introduce a few goldfish.

If the plants are to be of prime importance in a conservatory or garden room, the flooring should be as practical as possible. Ceramic tiles are often used for effect, but these must have a non-slip surface with water likely to be lying about. Otherwise roughened concrete and paving slabs are probably the best materials. Vinyl flooring is not very satisfactory – it can be very slippery when wet, and water getting underneath will cause all kinds of problems. For the same reason, it is not a good idea to use upholstered furniture which could be damaged with the damp conditions generally prevailing. Treated wood, cane, aluminium and good quality plastic are possibly the most sensible.

Most conservatories can get very hot in summer. It is therefore essential to choose one with as good ventilation as possible, and some form of shading will be a necessity. Whitening the glass is successful, though not attractive, and can cause low light problems in bad weather. Blinds are probably the best answer. Whether these are Venetian, roller or cane will depend largely on taste and the style of the structure. There are even firms producing decorative chain curtains now – these look good and can be tied back on dull days. There is often a problem with taller conservatories of too much light coming through the roof where it may not be possible to fit blinds. One solution to this is to make a 'false ceiling' of plastic mesh which can be drawn across or back depending on the weather.

I do not propose to list every houseplant suitable for cultivation in the conservatory with some heat provided as much will depend on the orientation, and a selection can be made quite easily from the preceding sections of this book. There are, however, a few subjects I have purposely not mentioned so far because, although they are often sold as, and recommended for, home cultivation, owing to their habit they are much more suited to conservatory conditions, among these being many popular houseplant climbers.

The type of heating will largely depend on individual circumstances. Where the conservatory is very much a part of the rest of the home it is usually possible to extend the central heating to take it in as well, but often there is no fixed form of heating. In this case, though on cost grounds alone it is very much a second choice, the most efficient form of heating is the thermostatically-controlled greenhouse fan heater. Under no circumstances should other electrical forms of heating be installed because of the amount of moisture around.

***Abutilon striatum* 'Thompsonii'** is a fast-growing shrub with maple-like leaves spotted with yellow and orange flowers in late summer. To keep the plant bushy, it can be pruned back by about half in early spring.

Acacia armata is a curious shrub, with spiny cladodes (modified leaf stalks that look like leaves) and yellow, scented mimosa flowers in summer. *A. dealbata* is the florists' mimosa and is almost hardy in some parts of Britain. Both these plants will grow out-of-doors in summer and must have good ventilation. In winter enough warmth should be given just to prevent the plants from freezing.

Bougainvillea glabra is a climbing plant capable of becoming very large in time, and yet it is often sold, trained round a hoop, as a houseplant. It is best grown on a trellis, kept warm in summer and cool in winter, and pruned after flowering to keep it in bounds. There are some good cultivars available, such as *Bougainvillea* 'Mrs Butt'.

Oranges and **lemons** are very popular, though not all that easy to grow. For the best results you should go to a specialist nursery, and look for varieties suitable for conservatory growing in the United Kingdom, like *Citrus mitis*, a dwarf orange which makes a bush about 4 feet (1.2 m) tall and bears small bitter oranges, *C. sinensis*, which is spiny and has reasonable-sized palatable fruits, *C. limon* 'Meyeri' and 'Ponderosa' (dwarf forms of lemon tree), and *C. auriantum*, the Seville orange. Whitefly and greenfly are a problem and the bushes need regular treatment for this – make sure you use a spray which is suitable for use on food crops if you intend to eat the fruit. The bushes need full sun and soft water; they can be placed outside in a warm spot for the summer if desired.

Catharanthus roseus, the Madagascar periwinkle, is a dwarf, bushy plant with periwinkle-like flowers in several colours which is easily raised from seed and makes a useful front-of-the-bed plant. It is very easy to grow under conservatory conditions and may be kept from

Citrus mitis
(Calamondin orange)

year to year or discarded and replaced with fresh young plants annually.

Clerodendrum thomsoniae is a tall climber bearing balloon-like, white, papery flowers with a red tip. It is deciduous in winter and should therefore be given a rest at lower temperatures.

Clianthus, the lobster claw or parrot bill, is an unusual-looking plant with flowers of a shape and colour very much like a lobster's claw. There are two species sold as houseplants: *Clianthus formosus* is a bushy plant reaching about 2 feet (0.6 m); *C. puniceus* is a climber and best trained on a trellis.

Coffea arabica, the coffee plant, has dark shiny leaves and makes

99

quite a tall bush, but there is a dwarf form, 'Nana'. It can be produced by growing unroasted coffee beans, but under conservatory cultivation in Britain is unlikely to produce coffee beans itself.

Datura, or angel's trumpets, makes a large, bushy plant which has beautiful and gorgeously scented flowers, especially in the evening. *Datura suaveolens*, with white flowers, is the most commonly cultivated form; *D. candida* is similar but a better-shaped bush. *D. sanguinea* has orange-red flowers. Daturas can be raised fairly easily from seed, and should be pruned back after flowering to prevent the plants becoming straggly.

Gardenia jasminoides is another scented plant with lovely double white flowers and shiny green leaves. It needs a temperature differential of about 10°F (5°C) during winter when the flower buds are forming, and is therefore more satisfactory as a conservatory plant than a houseplant. Draughts, sudden temperature changes and dry air will cause the buds and flowers to drop off. Watering should be with soft, tepid water.

The glory lily, ***Gloriosa rothschildiana***, is a tuberous climbing plant with exotic, lily-like red and yellow flowers. There is another form, ***G. superba***, which is similar but the flower colour is different, starting green and changing through orange to red. After flowering, the watering is reduced and eventually stopped so the plant becomes dormant. The tuber is repotted for regrowth again in spring.

The indoor hibiscus, ***Hibiscus rosa-sinensis***, sometimes rather confusingly called rose of China, is a tender relative of our hardy garden plant. Where allowed to reach its full potential it makes a tall, bushy shrub with hollyhock-shaped flowers in several colours from spring to autumn. There is also a variegated form, 'Cooperi'.

The **hoyas** give people many problems as houseplants, and yet given the correct conditions in a conservatory they can be a delight. *Hoya carnosa*, the wax plant, is a strong climber reaching many feet in time. The pale pink, red-centred, scented, waxy flowers are produced in clusters throughout spring, summer and autumn. There is a smaller form, *H. bella*, which has white flowers and is more difficult to grow well; it is generally seen as a hanging pot plant. *H. carnosa* has a variegated form which is less rampant. The usual complaints about hoya are lack of leaves on the new shoots, and lack of flowers. The new stems are always bare at first, producing leaves later, and flower-lessness is usually caused by dead-heading, which also removes

Datura suaveolens (angel's trumpet)

the part of the plant producing next season's blooms.

Jacaranda mimosifolia is a ferny-leaved small tree, which does not generally flower indoors but can sometimes oblige in the conservatory. It can be raised from seed and must be watered with soft, tepid water.

There are two species of **jasmine** usually offered for sale for indoor cultivation, *Jasminum polyanthum*, the pink jasmine, and *J. primulinum*, the primrose jasmine, which, unlike the pink form, is not scented. Although these are usually obtained in forms where the training has

101

Jacaranda mimosifolia

been restricted, they are much better allowed to ramble through a trellis. To ensure the production of flowers, the plants should be given plenty of fresh air in summer and a cool winter temperature.

Musa paradisiaca is better known as the banana, and makes a large-leaved plant which is too big for many conservatories, although where there is room it is fun because it will actually produce good

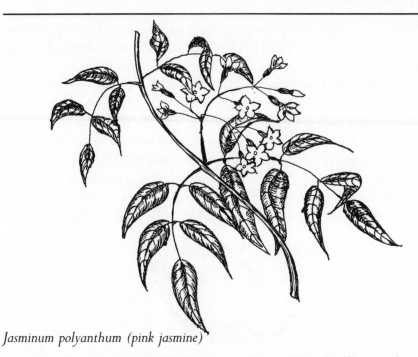

Jasminum polyanthum (pink jasmine)

bananas. The Canary Island banana (*M. acuminata*) is smaller, reaching about 6 feet (1.8 m), and in a light, humid situation will also produce bananas. Smaller than this, with yellow flowers and inedible fruit, is *M. velutina*; *M. coccinea* is smaller still, with red flowers and tiny ornamental bananas.

Nerium oleander, the oleander, is a beautiful plant when growing well, but it is difficult to get it to produce its large, fragrant, pink flowers – too much water in winter or too high a temperature and it will not bother. It likes plenty of fresh air in summer and can be put outside if practical, although as it makes a large bush this is not always so. In winter it likes a resting temperature of about 45°F (7°C). All parts of the plant are highly poisonous and should therefore be kept away from children, and pets which like to chew everything in sight.

Plumbago capensis, the cape leadwort, is a strong climber with heavenly blue flowers in summer. The plant can be pruned in winter and early spring to keep it in bounds. There is a white form which is pretty, though not as striking as the blue variety. *P. capensis* is often sold now under the newer name of *P. auriculata*.

Punica granatum, the pomegranate, makes a very big bush and is only really suitable for the larger conservatory. There is, however, a dwarf form, 'Nana', which has striking red tubular flowers, sometimes followed by miniature pomegranates, which do not usually ripen in this country. It is deciduous and can be stood outside in summer; the over-wintering temperature should be low but frost-free.

Stephanotis floribunda, the Madagascar jasmine, is a popular, though not always successful, climbing houseplant which thrives so much better under conservatory conditions. The flowers are white, not unlike the true jasmines, and are sweetly scented. It should be pruned back after flowering to encourage the production of flowering wood. It must be watered with soft water, and it detests draughts. Bud drop is usually caused by moving the plant while in flower, and can be prevented by using stephanotis as a permanent wall or trellis plant.

Stephanotis floribunda (wax flower, Madagascar jasmine)

Vallota speciosa, the Scarborough lily, is one of a number of bulbous plants with lily-like flowers in strong colours, such as **Clivia miniata**, the Kaffir lily, and **nerines**, which add a much needed splash of colour when grown in a conservatory. Cultivation is similar for all: a cool resting period after flowering (nerines will lose their leaves altogether for a time), and as little repotting as possible.

The unheated conservatory

Where no additional form of heating is provided, winter or summer, in a conservatory – except, perhaps, when the weather becomes exceptionally cold – the choice of suitable plants must be made very carefully. They will have to stand very low temperatures, be tolerant of fairly high ones in summer and be able to cope with a day/night differential of many degrees.

Possibly the best way of decorating an unheated conservatory is to use fairly hardy plants, especially those which are just not quite hardy enough to be able to recommend them for outdoor cultivation everywhere in the United Kingdom. Even quite hardy plants can be considered; their flowering season will be earlier, of course, than if they were growing in the open ground, but some might find excessively high temperatures in summer rather too much to cope with, in which case, wherever possible, they should be stood outside. Also it must be remembered that they are likely to grow larger and faster with glass protection.

Temporary colour

Temporary colour can be introduced in spring and summer by potting-up garden annuals, both hardy – like **calendulas, love-in-a-mist, larkspur, night-scented stocks**, annual **chrysanthemums** – and half-hardy – **antirrhinums, stocks, French marigolds, asters, salvias**, and so on. These are sown into seed trays in a warm, light position in the usual way, and potted-on into individual pots, troughs, baskets and the like; hardy forms will make good plants if a very small pinch of seed is germinated in a 3½-inch (9-cm) plant pot and allowed to reach maturity without transplanting. If you wish to grow half-hardy annuals and you do not have anywhere warm to raise them, you can buy young plants from the garden centre or wait until the temperature has warmed up sufficiently in the conservatory before sowing.

Talking of temporary decoration, bulbs are always useful. Winter bulbs will flower much longer where no artificial heat is provided, and there are many half-hardy, summer-flowering forms which would give a good display in this kind of situation. Among these are **freesias**; **Acidanthera murielae**, with white, purple-centred flowers; **Brodiaea laxa**, which has agapanthus-shaped heads of blue flowers on dainty stems and is reasonably hardy; **Canna hybrida**, with lily-like flowers in red or orange and large, showy, dark-coloured oval leaves; **Eucomis comosa**, the pineapple lily, which has white, pineapple-shaped flower heads; **Ipheion uniflorum**, with campanula-like blue flowers in early spring when grown under glass; **Ixia hybrida**, the African corn lily, which looks like a miniature gladiolus; **butterfly gladioli**; **Ornithogalum thyrsoides**, the chincherinchee, with fragrant white flower spikes; **Sparaxis tricolor**, the harlequin flower; **Tritonia crocata**, another gladiolus-shaped flower similar to ixia; and the calla lily, **Zantedeschia aethiopica**, with fragrant white, arum-like flowers in spring.

Most lilies will also thrive in a well-ventilated greenhouse if potted up in lime-free compost and not allowed to dry out. Especially acceptable are those with scented flowers, like the yellow **Lillium auratum, L. longiflorum**, the white Easter lily, **L. regale**, the white regal lily, and the Mid-century Hybrids such as **'Enchantment'** (orange), **'Destiny'** (lemon), **'Brandywine'** (apricot), and **'Tabasco'** (dark red).

Another member of the lily family, **Agapanthus africanus**, makes a good conservatory plant when it does not always do very well out-of-doors. This has ball-shaped heads of blue or white flowers with strap-like leaves. The bulbs will flower better if pot-bound and if planted in John Innes No. 2 compost should not need to be repotted unless the container becomes full to bursting point.

Permanent planting

It is the shrubs of slightly questionable hardiness, however, which make up the backbone of a cold conservatory permanent planting, so I will briefly describe those I have found to be among the most successful.

Abelia X grandiflora makes a bushy plant which is semi-evergreen when grown under glass. It has slightly scented, white and pink flowers tinted purple, and there is a particularly attractive variegated form, 'Frances Mason'. **A. schumanni** has lilac-rose, bell-shaped flowers.

Abutilon megapotanicum will make a large shrub, but trains well against a wall. It has lantern-shaped orange and yellow flowers from spring onwards. *A. vitifolium* 'Suntense' has vine-like, downy leaves and bluish-mauve, hollyhock-like flowers.

Many rhododendrons are of questionable hardiness in the United Kingdom, but often make small trees in time, so are not really suitable for the majority of conservatories. However, their close relation, *Azalea japonica*, the Japanese azalea, is a very small shrub, and whereas it will survive in the garden in all but the most inclement situations, some forms are less hardy than others, and will make good indoor specimens where there is no additional heating.

Boronia, a genus of half-hardy Antipodean shrubs, is sometimes found for sale in garden centres in the south of England in spring. The variety usually offered is 'Brown Meg', which has delicate, fine foliage and odd, brown, bell-shaped flowers with a delightful scent. Boronia will definitely show signs of unhappiness if it encounters more than a degree or so of frost.

Callistemon citrinus, the bottlebrush plant, is easy to grow under cold glass and makes a bright splash of colour with its bottle-brush-shaped, bright red flowers. When it begins to get 'leggy' it can be pruned back in early spring.

Camellias are definite favourites for the cold conservatory, although sometimes they are easier to grow outside except in very harsh conditions. Most forms sold for garden cultivation are cultivars of *Camellia japonica*, which are quite hardy in nearly all areas and like very cool conditions in winter. They benefit from being outside in summer; the buds form in July and August so on no account must they be allowed to dry out then or they will abort next year's flowers. Camellias kept under glass in winter will flower earlier than those outside. They should not be given a rapid change of temperature – from cold to warm – during the flowering period or they will shed their buds and flowers and quite possibly their leaves as well. Soft water should be used where it is available, and the plants should be potted in ericaceous compost. If the leaves gradually turn yellow, it is a sign of iron or magnesium deficiency, which can be corrected by watering the roots with sequestrene of iron.

Carpenteria californica is a tall, bushy evergreen which is only suitable for larger conservatories, but in the right situation makes a decorative bush with large, white flowers with yellow anthers in June. A position with a lot of sun is essential.

Ceanothus, the Californian lilac, is seldom seen as a conservatory subject, and yet it is extremely attractive as such, whereas in the open garden it generally needs wall protection, and even then can be severely damaged by cold. The clear blue flowers are borne in spring or late autumn, depending upon variety. 'A. T. Johnson' blooms at both ends of the year. *C. dentatus* and *C. impressus* are similar, with small, serrated, glossy green leaves; the flowers, which are produced in spring, are darker in *C. impressus*. *C. veitchianus* has intense blue flowers which appear in large numbers. All the ceanothus listed above are fully evergreen under cold glass conditions.

Scented shrubs are always useful, and there are two which are appreciative of some protection during colder conditions that will fill the whole structure with fragrance in spring. One is **Chimonanthus praecox**, the winter sweet. This will flower from December in a conservatory, with purple-centred ivory flowers. The variety 'Grandiflorus' is a deeper colour; 'Luteus' is yellow, without any purple. The other 'must' for scent is **Daphne odora 'Marginata'**. This is a well-shaped, medium-sized bush with cream-margined leaves and a delicious perfume in spring from clear pink flowers. There are other daphnes which could be used in the same way, but this particular one makes the best-looking specimen for this type of situation.

Most clematis would find the temperature in summer in an unheated conservatory rather too much, but there is an evergreen species, which sometimes struggles outdoors, that makes a good cool glasshouse plant. That is **Clematis armandii**, an early-flowering form with waxy white flowers in April and large, three-lobed, glossy leaves. It is ideal for a trellis on the back wall of a lean-to type of construction.

Desfontainea spinosa is a difficult evergreen out-of-doors, but if given cold conservatory protection it will make a good-looking bush with holly-like leaves and scarlet and yellow, trumpet-shaped flowers from July. It prefers lime-free compost, a partially shaded position, and a fair amount of humidity.

Under glass, hardy winter-flowering heathers will make a fine display throughout winter, but there are two **ericas**, *Erica hyemalis*, the French heather, and *E. gracilis*, the Cape heath, which are not hardy in most parts of Britain and are therefore sold as flowering houseplants.

They are both pinkish in colour; the French heather has bigger flowers. You may also sometime come across the Christmas heather, *E. hymalis*, which is white-flowered, and *E. ventricosa*, a midsummer-flowering species with mauve or white flowers. These heathers are difficult to grow indoors as the air is usually too warm and dry, but make excellent conservatory subjects, where they can be kept from year to year by cutting the plants back after flowering and standing the pots outside during summer. Watering must always be with soft water.

Most forms of evergreen **euonymus** are planted as foliage shrubs in the garden, but there are a few species which can sometimes be damaged during a hard winter and these benefit from cool conservatory cultivation. Among these are the gold and green-variegated, narrow-leaved *Euonymus japonicus (ovatus)* 'Medio-pictus', and the larger, rounder leaved *E. japonicus microphyllus* 'Albus', which has white and pale cream variegations. Other plants coming into this same category of benefiting from a bit of shelter are many of the large-leaved **hebes**, often named cultivars of the purple-racemed *Hebe speciosa*, for example 'Gauntlettii' (red and purple), 'La Seduisante' (crimson), and 'Veitchii' (purple-blue). *Hebe salicifolia* can also be damaged by frost, and given glass protection will make a much better bush of large, willow-shaped, pale green leaves and long racemes of violet-tinted white flowers. *Hebe elliptica* 'Variegata' is a much smaller plant, with cream-variegated, rounded leaves and short, violet racemes. It often browns in winter outside in colder areas.

If you are looking for a tall, eye-catching specimen plant, you could do worse than plant a **eucalyptus**. Two forms are commonly used for conservatory decoration, *Eucalyptus gunnii*, the species most widely seen as a garden shrub or small tree, which is hardy in Britain in all but the worst winters, and *E. globulus*. This latter is not generally hardy, but grows rapidly to make a very large plant in a short time. It is easily raised from seed, so older plants can be discarded if preferred, although they can be pruned back to give a multi-branched shrub. It is interesting to note that the juvenile foliage of the eucalyptus is quite different in colour and form, and generally thought to be more attractive, than that of mature plants, so it is advisable for the best effect to keep cutting all forms of eucalyptus hard back annually in spring.

A cold conservatory is a first-class place to grow many forms of slightly tender **fruit**, for example figs, peaches, nectarines, apricots and grapes. Figs make bushy plants if root-contained in tubs, and produce their fruit much earlier in life. Possibly the variety 'Brown Turkey' is still one of the best for quality and flavour. Peaches and similar fruit are best grown in fan-trained form on a solid wall, although where the conservatory is free-standing, those grafted onto dwarfing rootstocks and recommended for patio cultivation will make reasonable bush specimens when grown in large tubs of John Innes No. 3 compost. Cultivars suitable for outdoor culture will also thrive under cold glass. The most widely available varieties, and also the easiest to grow with a good flavour, are for peaches: 'Amsden' (early), 'Peregrine' (mid-season) and 'Barrington' (late); for nectarines: 'Early Rivers' (early), 'Lord Napier' (mid-season) and 'Pine Apple (late); for apricots: 'Farmingdale' (early to mid-season) and 'Moorpark' (late). Peaches, nectarines and apricots grown under glass may need hand-pollinating on warm days when the flowers are fully open; leaving the conservatory doors and windows open will encourage pollination by insects. The most reliable and well-flavoured grape is perhaps 'Black Hamburg' – this is best trained as a single rod along the highest part of the conservatory. A grapevine will throw a lot of shade in summer when in full leaf, which is beneficial to many plants being grown underneath, especially where artificial shading is inadequate, but you should avoid planting sun-lovers and vines together for obvious reasons.

Another food plant which can be used for indoor cultivation is **passiflora**. The variety grown primarily for its distinctive passion fruits is *Passiflora edulis*; this is not as decorative as other forms grown for purely ornamental purposes, such as *P. coerulea* and *P. quadrangularis*. All forms make large climbers in time, and flower and fruit better when grown in slightly starved and root-contained conditions. They are, even so, likely to put a lot of growth on before they get round to doing anything else, so it is advisable to choose the position with care, as cutting back will only produce green growth, and will not promote the production of flowers.

While still on the subject of things edible, the sweet bay, *Laurus nobilis*, is an ideal cold conservatory shrub. It responds well to clipping into a variety of ornamental shapes and forms, the clippings being useful in both fresh and dried form as a flavouring for many dishes. Bay trees are prone to aphid infestation; where this is severe sooty mould can occur on the secretions of these pests. They can be controlled by spraying with a pesticide suitable for glasshouse crops –

the sooty mould, where it is a problem, is best dealt with by being washed off.

A houseplant appearing more and more in garden centres in spring is **genista**, which is really a slightly tender form of broom, usually *Cytisus canariensis*, or sometimes *C. racemosus*. There are characteristic yellow, pea-like, heavily scented flowers in spring, after which the plants should be cut back (but not into old wood), and preferably stood outside, or in another light, cool, airy spot, until brought inside again in the autumn.

Two foliage shrubs which make good indoor decoration are **griselinia** and **pittosporum**. In some parts of the country, mainly in coastal situations, most forms of these plants are just hardy, but grow much better with some protection. *Griselinia littoralis* is a large shrub which responds well to regular pruning. Its variegated form is less strong-growing, with cream-variegated leaves. There are several species of pittosporum which are suitable for the conservatory; the one usually sold as a houseplant is *Pittosporum tobira*, sometimes called mock orange, which is a small, bushy plant with leathery leaves and small, white, fragrant flowers. There is also a variegated form of this species. *P. tenuifolium* is usually found among the outdoor plants for sale at nurseries and garden centres. It is a twiggy plant which gets quite large if not pruned, with apple-green, wavy-edged leaves much prized by flower arrangers. There is a more compact, white-variegated form which can become pink-tinged in winter, called 'Garnettii', and some specialist nurseries have other species available if you are looking for a conservatory plant with a difference.

Hydrangea macrophylla, the mop-head hydrangea, is often sold as a houseplant, but in fact grows perfectly well outside. However, plants grown under glass will flower much earlier, and often produce better heads, where they are not having to do battle with the elements. If the leaves begin to lose colour, a dose of Epsom salts watered onto the roots or sprayed on as a foliar feed will usually green them up.

Myrtus communis, the fragrant myrtle, with its sweetly scented white flowers in late summer, is hardier than many people imagine, but benefits from glasshouse protection; the confined environment also gives you the opportunity of getting the most benefit of the fragrance. A related species from the same family, *Leptospermum scoparium*, requires similarly sheltered conditions. The cultivar 'Kiwi' has jewel-like dark red flowers and small-leaved, bronzy foliage. *L. nanum* 'Huia' has pink blossom. 'Red Damask' has cherry-red, fully double flowers; those of 'Snow Flurry' are large, double and white. Both myrtle and most leptospermums will become quite large bushes but are happy being pruned back in spring.

Much of the attraction of a collection of plants in a conservatory is the way they are put together, blending and contrasting flower and foliage forms and colour. A handy species with which to introduce different shapes and leaf colour is **phormium**, the New Zealand flax. The all-green, widely planted form, *Phormium tenax*, which has red flower spikes on it in some summers, is pretty tough and too big and unwieldy for indoor cultivation, but there are some cultivars, such as 'Dazzler', 'Maori Sunrise', 'Purpureum' and 'Sundowner', which do not grow as large and have leaves spectacularly variegated with red, pink, apricot and purple depending on variety. These phormiums are not as hardy, and planted outside you stand the risk of losing them, but they will provide interesting colour and texture under cold glass. There are other pretty variegated forms – *P. cookianum* 'Cream Delight' has leaves with a central splash of cream; *P. cookianum* 'Tricolor' is green, striped white, with a red margin.

I have mentioned one or two climbers suitable for these conditions already – there are a few others which are worthy of consideration where space allows. One is ***Jasminum officinale***, the summer jasmine, which is hardy, with dark green compound leaves and heavily scented white flowers all summer. It will grow quite satisfactorily under glass, where the scent can be almost overpowering. ***Trachelospermum jasminoides*** is rather more 'up-market' – a marginally hardy climber which grows better with protection. It has jasmine-like flowers in July and August, which are very fragrant; the leaves are evergreen, oval, dark and shiny. Another climber with a jasmine-like habit is ***Solanum jasminoides* 'Album'**, a fast-growing climber which is also evergreen and which produces loose clusters of white flowers with a yellow splash during the autumn. This, too, is questionably hardy out-of-doors, but is no bother in an unheated conservatory with enough room.

We should not, of course, forget **roses**, which can make quite good conservatory plants given the right conditions. There are many miniatures being sold these days as houseplants, such as 'Baby Darling', 'Yellow Doll', 'Starina' (vermilion-red), and 'Judy Fischer' (pink). These are usually bought in bud or flower and expected to behave

Scipus cernuus is a plant for those who tend to overwater *(previous page)*
The limefree compost of the indoor azalea must not be allowed to dry out *(above)*
Impatiens 'New Guinea Hybrids' is difficult to overwater *(below)*

The fragrant gardenia *(above left)* is a delightful plant for a heated conservatory
Hyacinths *(above right)* make a splash of spring colour in an unheated conservatory
The planted bowl *(below)* is a popular gift

Planting a bottle garden

Ingredients for a successful bottle garden *(above)*
Compost and charcoal are funnelled in *(below left)*
Suitable plants are inserted carefully through the neck *(below right)*

themselves under normal home conditions of heat, darkness and dry air. It is not surprising that the display is short-lived; miniature roses are just as hardy as any others which grow in our gardens and should be respected as such, giving them the lightest, coolest and airiest conditions possible and preferably planting them outdoors afterwards. Hybrid tea and floribunda roses can be grown in a cold conservatory, however, when they will flower much earlier than those out-of-doors, giving much-needed colour in spring. Again, they should have a spell in the fresh air if possible, and the coldest situation you can find during winter to give a period of rest. Perhaps the best varieties to choose are those which do not do very well in very cold winters, such as 'Whiskey Mac' and many of the yellow, older varieties of hybrid tea rose (for example, 'King's Ransom'). Climbing roses can also be used where there is a large, blank wall; again it is a good idea to choose those which benefit from glass protection, like 'Royal Gold', *Rosa banksiae* 'Lutea' and 'Mermaid'; these, too, are in varying shades of yellow.

It should not be forgotten, either, that all plants listed in the chapter on houseplants for unheated rooms would also be good candidates for the unheated conservatory. Cultivation in the latter environment would usually be easier than in the house. Watering is the greatest art, as much less will be needed at most times of the year than in the conservatory in which some heat is provided.

Terraria and bottle gardens

From reading other parts of this book, it must have become obvious that one of the most important factors governing the well-being of houseplants is the amount of moisture held in the air. Plants in general do not like a very dry atmosphere, but those which come from parts of the world naturally moist atmospherically take great exception to being subjected to air which contains little water – it places them under great strain as they are constantly giving out precious moisture from their leaves because of the natural transference of gaseous substances.

One way of improving the situation artificially is to grow plants in a small volume of air which becomes saturated with water much sooner. This is where the terrarium comes in. In its simplest form, it is a glass container which is totally enclosed on all sides – it has the advantages of keeping the air moist and of cutting down draughts, thus enabling plants susceptible to dry air and draughts to be grown more easily.

Possibly the earliest useful example of this method of cultivation was in the early 1800s, when Dr Nathaniel Bagshaw Ward, a butterfly collector amongst other things, discovered more or less by accident when collecting chrysalids how plants unsuited to a particular environment grew much better for much longer if provided with an enclosed situation. The doctor realized that, in addition to keeping butterfly pupae fresh, this was an ideal way of transporting plants around the world for long periods, and his discovery was to revolutionize the way plant collectors could bring back difficult species in good condition. The 'Wardian Case', as it came to be known, was the forerunner of the terrarium, which today, with the adversely dry environment of our modern homes, is becoming an increasingly popular way of cultivating certain types of plants.

The late 1980s' terrarium is an elaborate affair, many sided and with soldered or leaded glass, but to be successful, it need be no more than a glass fish tank with a transparent cover over it. Some of the containers being manufactured today have the terrarium very much more in mind than the well-being of the plants that will go in it – there are small, mirror-backed plant containers with a large proportion of glass missing in order to be able to plant them up, which are pretty useless for the purpose for which they were intended. The temptation here is to put them where you want to display them, rather than where the plant would prefer to live, and the missing glass cuts down the humidity greatly. Add to that the fact that they are generally much too small, and they soon amount to useless clutter. A terrarium, to function properly, must be large enough to contain its plants adequately, and the container must be able to create an enclosed microclimate.

However ornamental the structure may be, therefore, and however expensive, the fact remains that the most satisfactory terraria can be made from the simplest of containers. It is not even essential to use a glass structure – there are some excellent, inexpensive plastic ones around which do the job just as well. Even a goldfish bowl can be used to contain one or two plants.

The bottle garden is merely a variation on this theme – the earlier ones were made in carboys originally manufactured to contain acids and other chemicals. These were difficult to plant up because of the narrow neck, but improvised tools could be made by taping table forks and dessert spoons to the ends of long canes, and a tool for firming could be created by screwing a doorstop into the end of a bamboo cane. Nowadays these bottles are hard to come by, but there are new ones to be bought which are easier to plant as they have a wider neck through which you can easily get your hand. A large whisky bottle can be used to contain one or two plants, but here again you will have to make tools small enough to get through the mouth – the neck is very narrow.

The siting of the terrarium is important. It will need bright light in winter for most species, but should be out of very hot sunlight in summer which will tend to stew anything in it. Ferns and other green-leaved plants will grow in light shade – ferncases were very fashionable in the middle of last century. The purpose-made, green tinted bottles you often see offered for sale ready-planted will need more light than those made of clear glass, but, again, should not be allowed to get too hot.

When planting the bottle you must remember that, with luck, all plants will grow, and therefore it is better to under-plant than over-plant to allow room for growth, although I appreciate that a happy balance has to be struck between what is ornamental now, and what will look good some time ahead. You may have to prune the plants back somewhat if they begin to get out of hand. To get the most benefit from your plants for the longest period, young specimens can be used, but eventually, if everything grows well, and even if you have used the right plants, you will reach the time for a good clear-out. The open-topped terrarium is not quite as much of a problem as it is larger and easier to get into, but some drastic treatment will be necessary in time.

In a closed environment you should not use cacti and succulents, as the air will be too moist for them, and rotting off will probably occur. Where it is difficult to remove the spent blooms, it is also unwise to use flowering plants, as dropped petals and dead heads can set up rots which will spread to living tissue and cause die-back. In a Wardian case, terrarium or fish tank, however, it is possible to introduce some flowers, provided fading material is removed immediately. Where the atmosphere is very moist and humid, problems can also occur with woolly-leaved plants, which will be saturated with water and again can start to rot.

The principles of planting up the bottle garden and the terrarium are essentially the same. The glass must be scrupulously clean – I usually wash the container out with a solution of household bleach and water before rinsing it thoroughly and allowing it to dry completely. The bottom of the container is then covered with a 2-inch (5-cm) layer of washed pea gravel or granite chippings to assist the drainage; this depth may have to be adjusted in proportion for smaller containers. If the neck is narrow you may have to pour this through a cone made of stiff paper. On top of it is spread a thin layer of charcoal to sweeten the compost, followed by a 2-inch (5-cm) (or thereabouts) layer of good soil-less compost.

The average bottle holds about six small plants – these are planted next, using the dessert spoon, the table fork being used to tidy the compost after firming gently with the doorstop. Of course, if the bottle neck is wide enough, and in the case of the terrarium, the fingers can be used for this job. It is difficult to specify how many plants should be used in a terrarium or fishtank as it depends on its size, but spacings should be about 4 inches (10 cm) for slow-growing plants, and much more for more enthusiastic ones.

When choosing the plants, you should try to strike a balance between upright, compact and trailing plants, so you achieve a landscape in miniature; the taller plants will be positioned in the centre of a container designed to be viewed from all angles, and to the back of a one-sided display. The compost in a bottle garden will have to be flat because of the limited soil surface, but in the larger terrarium and fish tank it can be mounded up in places to create a miniature landscape, and rocks can be introduced to add to this effect.

Plants suitable for this kind of cultivation are **ferns** (see page 70), especially *adiantum*, the maidenhair fern, *Pteris*, the table fern, and *Didymochlaena truncata*, the cloak fern; **cryptanthus**, the earth star, a flat-growing bromeliad which likes very humid air; ***Dracaena sanderiana***, a slow-growing species (see page 50 for other varieties) with green and white-variegated leaves which is useful as a taller-growing 'accent' plant; ***Ficus pumila*** (see page 71); **fittonia** (see page 75); small-leaved, slower growing varieties of ***Hedera helix***, such as 'Little Eva', which may need severe pruning in time; maranta (see page 71); young **palms** such as *Chamaedorea elegans* (these may eventually grow too large, but are useful as a central focus); ***Pellionea daveauana*** and

Maranta leuconeura 'Kerchoveana' (prayer plant, rabbit's foot)

117

P. pulchra, two green-leaved foliage plants which do not like draughts but will grow in shade; **Hypoestes sanguinolenta 'Splash'**, a newer and particularly well-marked form of the polka-dot plant, which has green and pink-spotted leaves and is easily raised from seed; **pilea** (see page 89); **crotons** (see page 50); and **selaginella**. This last is a moss-like plant which is difficult to grow in the home because it hates a dry atmosphere but is reasonably happy in the humid confines of the terrarium and bottle garden. *S. kraussiana* 'Aurea' is a low-growing form with a yellowish-green mossy leaf and a spreading habit. *S. uncinata* is blue-green and trailing. *S. martensii* is taller (12 inches) and suitable for larger terraria; *S. emmeliana* is another upright-growing species but about half as tall.

After planting up, the compost should be watered until it is just damp. Where it is difficult to get the spout of the watering can close to the surface (as in the case of bottles with very narrow necks), it may be necessary to trickle the water down the side – above all, you should be careful not to wash the compost away from the newly-planted specimens. It is wise to leave the bung or cork out, the cover off the fish tank, and the access door of the terrarium open for a week or so until the garden settles down. (Some terraria have one section left permanently unglazed; these will need watering in the future more often than those which are totally enclosed. Sealed gardens, in theory, should not need watering again.) Once the bung is replaced or the cover put into position, the plants should get to work to make their own stable micro-environment, but occasionally, usually if the compost is rather too damp, condensation may occur, in which case the garden should be opened up again to allow it to evaporate.

Over-wet compost is the most common cause of failure, as the plants will rot off. Too much sunshine will also cause problems, as will allowing dead, dying and diseased material to remain. It can be difficult to remove this debris where the access is restricted – you may have to resort to lifting it out with two canes, rather like using chopsticks!

The ready-planted bottle and terrarium are available from many stores and garden centres these days – while it is nice to have a ready-made feature with all the work done for you, it has to be said that many of the plants included have been selected, not so much for suitability, but for cost and effect and do not make good bottle-garden subjects. Unless you are sure about their appropriateness, it is often better, and undeniably more satisfying, to do the job yourself.

Novelties and gimmicks and what to expect from them

Cultivating plants in the home does not, by any means, end with just buying a houseplant in the garden centre or supermarket and finding somewhere suitable to put it when you get it home. The gardening press and broadcasters tell us that the possibilities of growing more weird and wonderful things every week are limitless, and the defence-less gardener is increasingly being bombarded with novelty products to bring more fun into inside gardening, so in my final section I am going to take a brief look at popular suggestions and what is around and give my honest opinion of what you can expect.

Growing herbs and vegetables on the windowsill
Most popular culinary herbs – mint, parsley, sage, thyme, basil, chives, rosemary, oregano and bay, for instance – will grow reasonably well on a sunny window ledge, and will remain green over winter, ensuring there is a constant supply when needed. The herbaceous kinds do not make the tidiest houseplants and need regular picking to prevent them becoming straggly. You really need at least two pots of each, so one can be allowed to recover while you use the other. The light has to be good because otherwise they will become drawn and 'leggy', especially in warm rooms.

There are certain salad vegetables and similar, such as tomatoes, peppers, aubergines, cucumbers and okra, which are quite successful when grown in the home, providing you have a light window which is large enough to accommodate the plants without blocking out most of the light, as even the more restrained forms get quite tall. Choose dwarf forms which have been specially bred with house cultivation in mind and treat them exactly as you would if growing them in a normal greenhouse. Look for suitable varieties like tomato F_1 hybrid 'Totem', sweet pepper F_1 hybrid 'Redskin', cucumbr F_1 hybrid 'Fembaby', aubergine 'Easter Egg', capsicum (hot pepper) 'Cayenne Hot'; and okra 'Clemson Spineless'. Plants such as these grown in the rather stuffy atmosphere of the home can be prone to pests and diseases – good ventilation is needed, as is spraying with a glasshouse crop insecticide at the first signs of insect attack.

The planted bowl

Buying a small bowlful of young houseplants has become an increasingly popular way of making a gift, and larger garden centres usually have a selection of these to choose from at all times of the year. They are, in general, only a temporary arrangement, as the bowls do not usually have drainage holes so watering is tricky, and where the bowl has already been planted the combinations of species are more for aesthetic effect than environmental compatibility. Some of the more enlightened nurseries will make up arrangements of this kind on the spot for you, so if you have some idea of which plants like similar situations, you can choose a selection of these.

If you acquire a bowl containing species liking different conditions, ideally the individual plants should be repotted immediately you receive the bowl and given the spots they prefer, but if this is not convenient, the best compromise is to place it in a good light out of direct sunlight, in which position most plants will grow reasonably well, in the short term, anyway. For good effect the bowls are always packed with plants, so they will have to be repotted fairly soon as they will rapidly become overcrowded, losing condition and becoming misshapen. The planted bowl is an attractive gift and much better value than, say, a bouquet of flowers, but much more expensive usually than buying the same plants individually as you are also paying for the bowl and the making up.

Growing houseplants from seed

Some houseplants, like grevillea (see page 79), zonal pelargoniums (see page 44), busy lizzies (see page 51), coleus (see page 43), cineraria (see page 59), cyclamen (see page 59), asparagus (see page 58), cacti (see page 41), celosia (see page 43), hypoestes (see page 118), peppers (see page 44), primulas (see page 79), saintpaulia (see page 55), solanum (see page 44), streptocarpus (see page 56) and succulents (see page 42), are comparatively easily grown from seed, and this is quite often how the nurseryman produces his plants, especially those grown for their flowers. Some seed companies offer seed for species requiring a considerable amount of skill to germinate and grow on successfully, such as banana (see page 102), bromeliads (see pages 45 and 81), ficus (see pages 60 and 71), palms (see page 71) and pineapple (see page 45). While it is by no means impossible to raise this type of houseplant in this way, the results are variable, germination can be erratic, and the growing conditions must be exactly right. It is possible to reproduce these conditions in the home by using correctly facing windowsills, but for the types more easily grown from seed, where the germination rate is high, a greenhouse or conservatory is usually necessary to enable the seedlings to have enough space to develop properly.

Ti-trees

I have already touched on this topic briefly on page 47. A ti-tree is the plant that develops when pieces of mature, woody stem from the dracaena, cordyline or yucca are planted, producing a palm-like crown of leaves from somewhere near the top. It is also the name given to an old dracaena, cordyline or yucca which has been sawn off somewhere down the trunk and which has sprouted again.

When making a ti-tree from a piece of unrooted trunk or cane, the base is inserted firmly into peat-based potting compost which is kept damp, but not wet. Rooting should occur, and a little later the new leaves will start to appear, but this can take several months. If the cane rots, the compost has been overwatered.

Ti-canes, which are small pieces of similar plants imported from abroad and dried before shipment, are becoming popular 'novelty' items at garden centres. The usual instructions are to scrape the wax protective coating from the base of the cane, which is often marked in some way to avoid confusion, and insert it in a shallow bowl of water. There are even kits available comprising a piece of dried cane, a few pebbles or chippings to give support while the end is in water, and a small glass bowl. Results with these ti-canes vary considerably from fairly successful to complete disaster, with the cane rotting off. Although this is often due to the water not being changed enough, I feel that water culture can be fraught with danger anyway, and growing a ti-cane is still more successful if damp compost is used instead. Because the cane is dry, it can take a very long time for anything to happen.

Tissue culture plants

These are very much a gimmick of the 1980s. I have already explained briefly on page 8 the principles of micro-propagation, and whereas so far it has not been a successful home propagation technique, it is theoretically possible to grow the very small plants produced by tissue culture without any special equipment or environment. Several firms have now made available to the amateur these very tiny plants, complete with instructions on how to grow them on into normal houseplants.

The kit they offer generally consists of the baby plant in a sealed phial of nutrient jelly. The stage at which the plant is at the moment of planting is critical to its subsequent success or failure, as there must be a young, healthy root system showing before it is taken out of the phial if it is to survive. The plant is removed from the phial by washing it out with clean, tepid water to prevent damage to the delicate young leaves, and is potted up in a very tiny pot of best quality houseplant compost. A mini-greenhouse is created by covering the pot with a jam jar or tumbler for a few weeks until there are visible signs of growth. The plants should be given a light position but with no direct sunlight or they will cook under the jar. It is an interesting, though not necessarily less expensive, way of acquiring houseplants, but the failure rate for most people is quite high. The choice is limited, but more micro-propagated plants are becoming available; among those readily obtainable are orchids, banana, pineapple, passionfruit and coffee.

Rose of Jericho

Another curiosity often picked up by casual garden-centre shoppers is *Seleginella lepidophylla*, better known as the resurrection plant or rose of Jericho. It will not contribute much to the overall effect of your living room, but children find it fun and when you have never had dealings with this plant before it is quite fascinating. It is bought as a hard, dry ball of scaly leaves and flat branches. Pop it into water and the ball uncurls into a flat rosette of green foliage!

Insect-eating plants

To me there seems to be something rather sinister about most insectivorous plants, but perhaps this is because their leaves are so strangely modified to cope with their unusual way of feeding. In the wild, these plants grow where the soil is so poor that they cannot obtain enough nourishment from it to survive. In a way they are like bromeliads in that they have to resort to a kind of foliar feeding, but whereas a bromeliad generally uses the centre of the plant to trap water, dissolved nutrients dropping from above and the odd suicidal insect, the insect-eating plants take more direct action to grab a bite to eat.

Insectivorous plants do not make very good houseplants as they need a very humid, warm environment, a permanently moist, lime-free compost, and watering with soft water at all times. There is also the temptation to overfeed with tiny bits of raw, fresh (not cured) meat or dead flies, but the requirements of these plants is quite low and they only need the occasional morsel.

Insectivorous plants come in three groups – those which trap insects with spiny-edged leaves having a hinged middle to close the leaf around its prey, such as that most popular of all insect eaters the Venus fly-trap (*Dionaea muscipula*), those which have hairy leaves which excrete a sticky substance to 'glue' the prey onto them, for example the sundews (**drosera**)'; and those which have leaves modified to form pitchers. These pitchers contain a digestive solution, and usually have hinged lids or hoods to prevent the trapped insect, which is usually lured in there by the marking on the throat, from crawling out again. Examples are *Darlingtonia californica*, *Nepanthes coccinea*, and *Sarracenia drummondii*.

Apart from the Venus fly-trap, obtaining these plants is usually a matter of going direct to a handful of growers who specialize in insectivorous species. They often exhibit at larger flower shows and in the exhibition tents of agricultural shows. With an increasing demand for these unusual plants, however, the better-known species such as those mentioned above can sometimes be found at garden centres with a large houseplant section. They are expensive, though, and unless you have a greenhouse or conservatory with the right conditions, they do not usually survive very long.

Indoor bonsai

Bonsai is the Japanese art of dwarfing and training trees, usually hardy, to create an old and gnarled appearance. In a way it is like living sculpture, and, like this art, you either like it or you don't; even those who feel it is a mutilation of a living, growing thing cannot help but be impressed with some bonsais, perhaps many, many years old, which recreate a wild landscape in perfect miniature. The dwarfing process is brought about by regular pruning and pinching back of the top growth and annual root pruning. The shape is developed by weighting the branches or wiring them so that they start to grow a certain way.

Bonsai is an art learned and improved upon through years of experience and the various methods are beyond the scope of this book, but others specializing in the art are in the list of recommended reading on page 128.

Bonsai trees are always grown in an open, soil-based compost in shallow, ceramic pots without drainage holes, and most woody species are suitable for treatment this way. Most bonsais are obtained as young specimens already partly trained, but there is no reason why you should not start your own from scratch with a small seedling. There is no point in buying the very expensive bonsai starter kits which comprise little more than a few tree seeds, a flat plastic container and a bit of compost, as you can dig up small seedlings of trees such as oak, birch, beech, maple and sycamore and get to work on these (but do obtain permission from the owner of the land first, of course!).

The point which is not generally appreciated is that nearly all bonsais are completely hardy in Britain, and therefore should not be used as houseplants, except for a very short period. They should live outside in the same environment that they would grow in naturally, only being given protection during very cold spells – this can be done without having to move them inside by covering them with straw temporarily. Garden centres often add to the confusion by displaying their selection of bonsais with the houseplants – this will not have done them much good, so if you intend to buy one, try to obtain it from a nursery where they are kept outside, or deal with a specialist.

Bonsais can add much to the interior decor, and in recent years tender specimens have become available, which are suitable for light positions in the home. As with other tender species grown as houseplants, the environment should be the prime consideration; a tender bonsai tree is no more likely to thrive in an unsuitable place than any other houseplant.

Trees and shrubs which you are likely to see grown as indoor bonsais are *Ficus benjamina* (weeping fig), *Sageretia theesans*, *Pistacia terebinthus* (pistachio), *Punica granatum* (pomegranate), *Olea europaea* (olive) and *Jasminum primulinum* (primrose jasmine). These are cultivated and trained in the same way as hardy bonsais. The watering has to be watched carefully, as the compost can easily dry out in the shallow container, but care must be taken not to overwater because of the lack of drainage holes in some bonsai pots.

Growing pips, stones and nuts

There is a curiosity in most of us which prompts us to wonder what, if anything, will come up if we plant a nut out of the Christmas bowl, or a pip or stone from something we have just eaten. It is easy to produce plants in this way; all you need is some peat-based compost, a light windowsill and some patience. What is less certain, though, is whether you are likely to get anything worthwhile at the end of the experiment, and this is more dubious.

Most pips and stones are from the fruit of very large trees and bushes, and will become too big in time for the average home. Also, it depends on the type of fruit you are trying to grow whether it will come true to type and if, when it outgrows its position on the windowsill, it will be hardy enough to grow outdoors. The following are the most popular pips, stones and the like, for germinating, and what you can expect to get.

Apples and pears germinate well, and grow rapidly indoors. The resultant plants are hardy in the United Kingdom, and should be put outside after a hardening-off period. They will make very large trees in time as they will not have the influence of the dwarfing rootstock onto which apple and pear varieties are grafted commercially. The resultant fruit will not be like its parent, and may be reasonable in quality or pretty mediocre. The same comment applies to **plums**.

Peaches grow extremely well from stones, and the plants usually produce very passable fruit in time. In warmer parts of Britain the bushes will be fairly hardy, especially if grown against a sunny wall, but better results are often obtained by growing in the greenhouse or conservatory. The fruit of seedling **nectarines** is variable, and that of **apricots** generally quite reasonable, but the apricot is less hardy and needs glasshouse protection.

Avocado stones germinate like weeds. Young avocado plants look rather like rubber plants. They soon get leggy, and if required for home decoration the growing points should be pinched out periodically. Avocados grown as houseplants do not generally produce avocado pears as the plants need to be fairly mature before fruit is formed, and mature avocados are quite large; however, in some taller conservatories there is a possibility of being able to harvest your own avocado pears. The seed of **mangoes** and **lychees** can be sown in a similar way and should produce interesting temporary houseplants or more permanent conservatory ones.

Lemon, orange, grapefruit and **lime** pips are old favourites for growing into plants. They make attractive bushes and will probably produce fruit in time, but the quality is variable and often the plants get too large for the home before this happens. Citrus plants need a lime-free compost and watering with soft water; they are very prone to whitefly and aphids and may have to be sprayed regularly to control these pests.

Grape pips also germinate easily. They will produce large vines quite rapidly which will need to be pruned while they are dormant (November to January – later than this causes the cuts to 'bleed' quite seriously) to keep them under control. Again, the resultant fruit tends to vary from quite good to rubbish. Grape vines grown from imported grapes will usually need greenhouse protection.

Pineapple plants can sometimes be persuaded to grow by cutting the top off a pineapple fruit having a healthy rosette of leaves, scraping away all the fleshy bits to leave a fibrous base to the leaves and, after allowing it to dry off for a few days, potting it up in peat-based compost. Roots will often form from below the leaves; if rotting occurs it is usually because the compost was too wet or the fleshy material was not thoroughly removed.

A simpler way to get something for nothing, although the plant which results will only be a temporary one, is to cut the top off a **carrot** or **parsnip** in late winter and then pot this up. It will soon grow into a bright green, feathery plant which will produce white umbels of flowers in summer. Children find this fun, and it can awaken in them an interest in growing things that may last a lifetime.

Date stones, pushed into compost, will grow and make very large palms, in time. Many a palm has been produced from a stone slipped into auntie's prize aspidistra after the Christmas lunch – much to the surprise of auntie and the annoyance of the aspidistra!

Children often find growing **peanuts** fascinating, and it is also an interesting experiment for anyone who has not seen the habit of the peanut plant. Fresh, unshelled nuts are pushed into a container of compost with a wide surface area – the nuts should be well-spaced because of the way the plant produces its nuts. A 12-inch (30-cm) high, rather insignificant plant will appear, which eventually flowers just above the surface. As the flowers fade, the stalks of the plant bend over to push the developing fruit into the compost, hence the peanut's other name – ground-nut.

As I said at the beginning of this section, the things we have just looked at are really more for interest than for their intrinsic beauty, although many of them can be absorbed quite well into a large collection of houseplants in, say, a conservatory, without them looking unsightly and cluttering up your window ledges. And if you've enjoyed finding out what comes up from what goes down, well – what the heck!

Further reading

The Gold-Plated Houseplant Expert, Dr D G Hessayon, Century.
Success With Houseplants, The Readers' Digest.
Cacti, Clive Innes, Cassell in conjunction with the Royal Horticultural Society.
Succulents, Clive Innes, Cassell in conjunction with the Royal Horticultural Society.
Indoor Bonsai, John Ainsworth, Ward Lock.
Bonsai, David Pike, Crowood Press.
African Violets, Tony Clements, David and Charles.
The Healthy Houseplants Handbook, David Squire, Michael Joseph.
Fuchsias (Kew Garden Guide), Hamlyn-Collingridge.
Geraniums and Pelargoniums, Jan Taylor, Crowood Press.
Pelargoniums (Collins Aura Guides), Pat Weaver, Collins.
The Complete Book of Orchid Growing, Peter Mckenzie Black, revised by Wilma Ritterhausen, Ward Lock.

Air plants (tillandsias) need the minimum amount of watering *(left)*
Primulas make good flowering plants for light, unheated rooms
Aechmea (urn plant) will take central heating in its stride *(overleaf)*